LOW CARB COOKBOOK
FOR BEGINNERS

Transform Your Health with Easy-to-Follow, Nourishing Meals:
Simple & Delicious Recipes for Newbies

Stefan Decker

TABLE OF CONTENTS

Introduction

Welcome to the "Low Carb Cookbook for Beginners", a culinary journey designed to integrate healthy eating seamlessly into your busy lifestyle. In today's fast-paced environment, nutritious eating often takes a backseat to tight schedules and demanding workloads. Yet, the key to optimal energy levels and overall well-being lies in the choices we make at the dining table. This cookbook serves as your ally in navigating the challenges of a busy lifestyle while harnessing the transformative power of low-carb eating.

In the pages that follow, we will explore the fundamental principles of a low-carb diet and introduce a variety of delicious recipes tailored for those just beginning their low-carb journey. But first, let's delve into the concept of low-carb eating and its myriad benefits, especially for individuals new to this way of life.

Understanding Low-Carb Eating

Embarking on a low-carb journey is more than a dietary change; it's a transformative approach to understanding how food influences your body's health and functionality. The cornerstone of low-carb eating lies in grasping the pivotal role carbohydrates play in our diets and their subsequent effects on our health. Carbohydrates, found in foods such as fruits, vegetables, grains and sugars, serve as the body's primary energy source. However, the impact of carbohydrates extends beyond mere energy provision; the quality and quantity of consumed carbs significantly influence bodily functions, weight management and overall health.

At its core, the science behind low-carb eating revolves around the body's carbohydrate metabolism. Consuming carbs leads to their breakdown into simpler sugars, mainly glucose, which then enters the bloodstream. This rise in blood sugar triggers the pancreas to release insulin, facilitating cells in absorbing glucose to be used as energy. Yet, an excessive intake of carbs, especially those derived from processed and sugary foods, can result in heightened blood sugar levels. Over time, this may contribute to insulin resistance, weight gain and an elevated risk of chronic conditions such as type 2 diabetes and heart disease.

By limiting carbohydrate intake, a low-carb diet aims to mitigate these health risks. Lowering carb consumption decreases blood sugar and insulin levels, encouraging the body to tap into stored fat for energy in a process known as ketosis. This not only aids in weight loss and management but also enhances metabolic health, offering a proactive stance against diabetes and other health issues.

Understanding carbohydrates involves differentiating among their types: sugars, starches and fiber. Sugars or simple carbohydrates, are quickly absorbed and found in fruits (as fructose) and processed foods (as sucrose or high-fructose corn syrup). Starches, complex carbohydrates, break down more slowly and are present in potatoes, grains and legumes. Fiber, another form of complex carbohydrate, remains indigestible and plays a vital role in digestive health. It is abundant in vegetables, whole grains and fruits.

Transitioning to a low-carb diet requires reducing high-carb food consumption, such as bread, pasta, rice and sugary snacks and prioritizing whole, unprocessed foods rich in proteins and healthy fats, including meat, fish and vegetables. This shift not only targets weight management and metabolic health improvements but also embodies a broader understanding and respect for the nutritional value of food, steering individuals towards making informed, health-conscious dietary choices.

Benefits for Beginners

Starting a low-carb journey can be a transformative experience, especially for beginners. This approach is not just about cutting back on certain foods; it's about discovering a new way to eat that can improve your health, energy and overall quality of life. Here's how beginners can particularly benefit from adopting a low-carb diet:

1. **Easy Start to Healthy Eating**: a low-carb diet simplifies the complex world of nutrition. By focusing on reducing carbohydrate intake and emphasizing proteins and healthy fats, beginners can make meaningful dietary changes without feeling overwhelmed.

2. **Sustained Energy Levels**: unlike diets high in carbohydrates, which can lead to blood sugar spikes and crashes, a low-carb diet helps maintain steady energy levels throughout the day. This makes it easier for beginners to stay focused on their tasks, whether at work, school or daily activities.

3. **Clarity and Focus**: reducing carbohydrate intake can also lead to improved mental clarity. Many beginners notice a reduction in the foggy-headed feeling often associated with high-carb meals, leading to better concentration and productivity.

4. **Effective Weight Management**: for those new to weight management, a low-carb diet offers a straightforward approach. By limiting carbs and focusing on protein and healthy fats, beginners can see sustainable weight loss results without counting every calorie.

5. **Reduced Cravings**: starting a low-carb diet helps curb cravings for sugary snacks and processed foods. Beginners often find it easier to stick to healthy eating habits when they're not constantly tempted by high-carb options.

Long-term Health Benefits: Adopting a low-carb lifestyle can have significant long-term health benefits, including improved cholesterol levels, reduced blood sugar and decreased risk of chronic diseases. Beginners setting off on their health journey can lay a strong foundation for a healthier future.

By focusing on these benefits, beginners can navigate their way through the initial challenges of adjusting to a low-carb diet and enjoy the positive changes it brings to their health and well-being.

Importance of a Balanced Diet for Beginners

Adopting a low-carb lifestyle marks a significant step towards health and well-being, especially for beginners on this journey. Yet, it's crucial to emphasize that the effectiveness of a low-carb diet hinges on more than just carbohydrate restriction; it requires a commitment to a balanced diet that nourishes the body with a wide spectrum of nutrients.

This holistic approach ensures that, while you're cutting down on carbs, you're not missing out on the essential vitamins, minerals and other nutrients that support overall health.

A balanced diet is characterized by variety and moderation, incorporating a broad range of foods from different groups to meet the body's nutritional needs. Proteins, fats and carbohydrates all play distinct and vital roles in bodily functions and a well-rounded diet includes healthy sources of each. For those embarking on a low-carb diet, it means prioritizing high-quality, nutrient-dense foods within the low-carb framework.

Proteins, the building blocks of muscles and tissues, should come from lean sources like poultry, fish, eggs and plant-based alternatives such as legumes and tofu. These sources not only support muscle growth and repair but also contribute to a feeling of fullness, which can help manage hunger and prevent overeating.

Healthy fats, contrary to outdated beliefs, are crucial for brain health, energy and the absorption of fat-soluble vitamins (A, D, E and K). Avocados, nuts, seeds and olive oil are excellent sources of monounsaturated and polyunsaturated fats. Incorporating these into your diet enhances cardiovascular health and provides sustained energy levels, making them indispensable in a low-carb diet.

While reducing carbohydrate intake, it's important to choose high-fiber, low-glycemic options that provide essential nutrients without spiking blood sugar levels. Vegetables, especially leafy greens and low-sugar fruits like berries offer vitamins, minerals, fiber and antioxidants that combat inflammation and support overall health.

Hydration is another critical aspect of a balanced diet, often overlooked in dietary planning. Water plays a key role in nearly every bodily function, including digestion and waste elimination. Adequate hydration can also aid in weight management by promoting satiety and reducing the likelihood of mistaking thirst for hunger.

Finally, a balanced diet acknowledges the importance of moderation and flexibility. Occasional treats and indulgences are part of a healthy, sustainable eating pattern, preventing feelings of deprivation that can derail long-term goals. For beginners, understanding that perfection isn't the goal – balance is – can be liberating and encouraging.

In summary, the importance of a balanced diet for beginners on a low-carb journey cannot be overstated. It's about making informed food choices that support a healthy lifestyle, ensuring adequate nutrient intake and maintaining an enjoyable, sustainable approach to eating. This balanced approach lays the foundation for achieving and maintaining health goals, enhancing the quality of life and fostering a positive relationship with food.

Chapter 1: Fundamentals of Low-Carb Eating for Beginners

In recent years, low-carb eating has surged in popularity as a method for weight management, improving metabolic health and boosting energy levels. This dietary approach focuses on reducing the intake of carbohydrates, a primary energy source for the body. Understanding the basics of low-carb eating is essential for anyone considering or already practicing this way of eating.

The Role of Carbohydrates in the Body

Carbohydrates play a multifaceted role in the human body, serving not only as the primary source of energy but also supporting various critical functions. When carbohydrates are consumed, the body breaks them down into simpler sugars like glucose, which is then distributed via the bloodstream to cells throughout the body. This glucose is vital for fueling brain activities, making it indispensable for cognitive functions such as thinking, memory and learning.

Additionally, during physical activities, carbohydrates provide the necessary energy to muscle cells, enabling both endurance and high-intensity performance. Beyond these roles, carbohydrates contribute to the body's overall well-being by supporting digestive health. Dietary fiber, a type of carbohydrate that the body cannot digest, helps regulate the body's use of sugars, helping to keep hunger and blood sugar in check. Fiber's presence in the diet aids in maintaining a healthy digestive system by promoting regular bowel movements and can contribute to lowering cholesterol levels, further protecting heart health.

Good vs. Bad Carbohydrates

Understanding the difference between good and bad carbohydrates is foundational for maintaining a healthy diet. Good carbohydrates are typically complex carbohydrates found in whole, unprocessed foods such as vegetables, whole grains, legumes and fruits. These carbohydrates are digested more slowly, leading to a gradual release of energy and a steady blood sugar level, which can help in maintaining energy levels and feeling full longer. They are also rich in nutrients and dietary fiber, contributing to overall health by providing essential vitamins, minerals and improving digestive health.

On the other hand, bad carbohydrates refer to simple carbohydrates and refined sugars found in processed foods, sugary drinks and snacks. These carbs are quickly absorbed into the bloodstream, causing spikes in blood sugar levels and often leading to energy crashes. Regular consumption of these high-glycemic index foods can increase the risk of health issues, including weight gain, diabetes and heart disease. They typically offer little nutritional value and are often high in calories, contributing to an unbalanced diet.

The Importance of Carbohydrate Quality in a Low-Carb Diet

Choosing high-quality carbohydrates is paramount in a low-carb diet, as it ensures the body receives essential nutrients while managing carbohydrate intake. High-quality carbs, such as those found in whole foods, are dense in nutrients and fiber. This not only supports the body's nutritional needs but also enhances satiety, which can aid in weight management. Incorporating these healthier carbohydrates helps minimize the negative impacts of carb reduction, such as nutrient deficiencies or digestive issues.

By focusing on the quality of carbohydrates, individuals can maintain a balanced and nutritious diet that supports long-term health and well-being, even within the framework of a low-carb eating plan. This approach to carbohydrate selection ensures that every carb consumed contributes positively to the body's nutritional needs, supporting overall health without compromising the goals of a low-carb diet.

Practical Tips for Reducing Carbohydrates

Adopting a low-carb lifestyle involves making conscious decisions to reduce carb intake while maintaining a balanced diet. Here are some practical tips for those embarking on a low-carb diet:

1. **Choose Whole Foods**: opt for whole, unprocessed foods such as vegetables, fruits, lean proteins and healthy fats. These provide essential nutrients without excessive carbohydrates.

2. **Read Food Labels**: pay attention to labels to spot hidden sugars and refined carbs. Avoid products with added sugars, white flour and other processed ingredients.

3. **Control Portions**: be mindful of portion sizes to manage overall carb intake. Consuming smaller, balanced meals can help regulate blood sugar levels.

4. **Explore Low-Carb Alternatives**: replace carb-heavy foods with low-carb alternatives. For instance, use cauliflower rice instead of traditional rice or lettuce wraps in place of bread.

5. **Stay Hydrated**: drinking water can help curb appetite and promote overall well-being. Sometimes, feelings of hunger can actually be signs of dehydration.

In conclusion, understanding the fundamentals of low-carb eating is crucial for successfully adopting this lifestyle. By being informed about carbohydrate quality, one can enjoy the numerous benefits of reduced carb intake, such as weight management, improved metabolic health and sustained energy.

Chapter 2: Planning Low-Carb Meals For Beginners

Techniques for Preparing and Storing Meals to Simplify Your Routine

In the journey of embracing a low-carb lifestyle, especially for beginners, understanding the basics of meal preparation and storage can make a significant difference. Establishing a routine that includes planning, preparing and storing your meals not only helps in adhering to a low-carb diet but also saves time, reduces stress and ensures that you have healthy options readily available. This chapter is designed to walk beginners through the fundamentals of meal planning and preparation. It will introduce you to techniques that simplify your meal routines and offer examples of appetizing low-carb menus that can fuel your body and mind with the necessary energy and nutrients.

Meal Preparation and Storage Techniques

1. **Meal Planning**: begin with the basics by planning your meals ahead. This helps in avoiding the temptation of reaching for high-carb options when you're unsure of what to eat.

2. **Batch Cooking**: spend a portion of your weekend preparing large batches of low-carb staples, such as grilled meats, roasted vegetables and hard-boiled eggs. This approach can save you considerable time during the week.

3. **Smart Storage**: invest in good quality storage containers to keep your prepared meals fresh. Labeling containers with the contents and the date prepared can help you keep track of what's ready to eat.

4. **Simplify with Slow Cookers and Instant Pots**: utilize kitchen gadgets like slow cookers and instant pots for making low-carb meals with minimal effort. These tools are especially useful for beginners who might not be confident in their cooking skills.

5. **Quick and Healthy Snacking**: keep a stash of low-carb snacks handy, such as nuts, cheese and pre-cut vegetables, to avoid high-carb temptations.

By applying these meal preparation and storage techniques, beginners can navigate their way through starting a low-carb diet with less hassle. Prioritizing your health and well-being by planning ahead enables you to enjoy the benefits of sustained energy and focus, making it easier to commit to a healthier lifestyle.

Examples of Weekly Low-Carb Menus

Day 1:
Breakfast: Protein-Rich Avocado Egg Cups
Lunch: Spicy Chicken and Roasted Vegetables
Dinner: Grilled Lemon-Herb Chicken with Zucchini Noodles

Day 2:
Breakfast: Berry Bliss Low-Carb Smoothie Bowl
Lunch: Cauliflower Bacon Soup
Dinner: Baked Salmon with Dill and Asparagus Spears

Day 3:

Breakfast: Spinach-Feta Omelette Roll-Ups

Lunch: Turkey and Vegetable Salad Wraps

Dinner: Cauliflower and Broccoli Alfredo Casserole

Day 4:

Breakfast: Keto-Friendly Chia Seed Pudding

Lunch: Grilled Shrimps and Avocado Salad with Lime Vinaigrette

Dinner: Spicy Shrimp Stir-Fry with Shirataki Noodles

Day 5:

Breakfast: Quick and Easy Bacon Egg Muffins

Lunch: Creamy Broccoli-Cheddar Soup

Dinner: Pesto Turkey Meatballs with Roasted Brussels Sprouts

Day 6:

Breakfast: Greek Yogurt Parfait with Nuts and Berries

Lunch: Stuffed Chicken Wraps with Mushrooms and Spinach

Dinner: Eggplant Lasagna with Turkey Minced Meat and Spinach

Day 7:

Breakfast: Zucchini Cheese Breakfast Casserole

Lunch: Spicy Chicken Caesar Salad

Dinner: Lemon-Garlic Butter Cod with Cauliflower Rice

Strategies for Quick and Healthy Lunches at Home or On-the-Go

1. **Salad Jars**: assemble your salad in jars, placing the dressing at the bottom to prevent wilting. When it's time to eat, simply shake the jar to enjoy a fresh and crisp salad.

2. **Wrap It Up**: opt for low-carb wraps or lettuce leaves as an alternative to traditional bread. Fill them with lean protein, vegetables and a tasty sauce for a fulfilling meal on the go.

3. **Smart Snacking**: keep a stash of healthy snacks like nuts, cheese and sliced vegetables at your desk to resist the temptation of office treats.

4. **Soup in a Thermos**: prepare a hearty low-carb soup and take it with you in a thermos. This is a warm and satisfying option that's easy to carry.

By applying these meal preparation and storage techniques, experimenting with various low-carb menus and implementing strategies for quick and healthy lunches in the office, you can successfully navigate the challenges of a low-carb diet during your busy workweek. Prioritize your health and well-being by planning ahead and enjoy the benefits of sustained energy and concentration throughout your workdays.

Chapter 3: Smart Shopping For Beginners

In today's fast-paced world, making smart decisions at the grocery store is crucial, especially when adopting a low-carb lifestyle. The supermarket can be a maze of options and navigating it with your health goals in mind requires strategic planning. This chapter delves into the art of smart shopping, providing a comprehensive guide for grocery shopping on a low-carb diet. A low-carb diet offers numerous health benefits, from weight management to improved blood sugar control. Intelligent shopping is a key aspect to ensure you have the right ingredients for your goals.

Guide to Low-Carb Grocery Shopping

1. **Prioritize Fresh Fruits and Vegetables**: focus on non-starchy vegetables like leafy greens, broccoli, cauliflower and bell peppers. These provide essential vitamins and minerals without significantly contributing to your carb intake.

2. **Choose Lean Proteins**: opt for lean meats such as chicken, turkey, fish and eggs. These protein sources are not only low in carbs but also provide vital nutrients for overall health.

3. **Navigate Dairy Aisles Wisely**: select full-fat dairy products like Greek yogurt, cheese and butter. These items contain fewer carbs than their low-fat counterparts and can enrich your meals.

4. **Stock Up on Healthy Fats**: include sources of healthy fats in your shopping list, such as avocados, nuts, seeds and olive oil. These fats are an essential part of a low-carb diet and contribute to satiety.

5. **Minimize Processed Foods**: limit consumption of processed foods, which often contain hidden sugars and unnecessary carbs. Stick to whole, unprocessed foods for the best results.

Tips for Reading Food Labels

1. **Check the Carb Content**: pay attention to the total carbohydrates per serving. Note that some products may contain hidden sugars or starches, so read labels carefully.

2. **Watch for Hidden Sugars**: look for various names for sugar, such as sucrose, fructose and corn syrup. Even seemingly healthy products can contain sugar additives that undermine your low-carb goals.

3. **Consider Net Carbs**: subtract the fiber from total carbohydrates to calculate net carbs, as fiber does not impact blood sugar levels. This gives you a more accurate representation of the carbs that affect your body.

Optimized Shopping List for a Balanced Low-Carb Diet

Proteins:

Chicken breast

Turkey

Fish (salmon, tuna)

Eggs

Vegetables:

Spinach

Broccoli

Cauliflower

Bell peppers

Dairy Products:

Greek yogurt (full-fat)

Cheese

Butter

Fats:

Avocados

Nuts (almonds, walnuts)

Olive oil

Extras:

Fresh herbs and spices

Unsweetened almond milk

Berries (in moderation)

Following this guide and tailoring your shopping list to your low-carb needs will make smart supermarket choices become second nature. With a well-stocked kitchen, you're not just buying food; you're investing in your health and well-being.

Chapter 4: Breakfast

1. Protein-Rich Avocado Egg Cups

Preparation Time: 15 minutes | Cooking Time: 15 minutes | Servings: 2

Ingredients:

- Avocados: 2 large, halved and pitted
- Eggs: 4 large
- Cooked turkey bacon: 1/2 cup, crumbled
- Feta cheese: 1/4 cup, crumbled
- Cherry tomatoes: 1/4 cup, diced
- Green onions: 1/4 cup, finely chopped
- Salt and pepper: to taste
- Fresh parsley: for garnishing

Instructions:

Preheat the oven to 200°C (392°F) or 180°C (356°F) for fan ovens.

Scoop out a small portion of the flesh from each avocado half to create a well for the egg.

Place the avocado halves in a baking dish to keep them stable.

Distribute the crumbled turkey bacon, feta cheese, diced cherry tomatoes and chopped green onions evenly among the avocado halves.

Carefully crack an egg into each avocado half, ensuring the yolk remains intact.

Season with salt and pepper to taste.

Bake:

Slide the baking dish into the preheated oven and bake for about 15 minutes, until the eggs are set.

Remove from the oven and garnish with fresh parsley.

Serve immediately and enjoy these protein-rich avocado egg cups!

Nutritional Values (per serving): Calories 350 | Fat 28g | Carbohydrates 9g | Protein 16g

2. Berry Bliss Low-Carb Smoothie Bowl

Preparation Time: 10 minutes | Cooking Time: 0 minutes | Servings: 2

Ingredients:

- Mixed berries (strawberries, blueberries, raspberries): 1 1/2 cups
- Unsweetened almond milk: 2/3 cup
- Greek yogurt: 1/2 cup

- Chia seeds: 2 tablespoons

- Protein powder (vanilla or berry flavored): 1/4 cup

- Almond butter: 2 teaspoons

- Low-carb sweetener (Stevia or Erythritol): 1 teaspoon

- Ice cubes (optional for a thicker consistency)

Instructions:

Combine the mixed berries, almond milk, Greek yogurt, chia seeds, protein powder, almond butter and low-carb sweetener in a blender.

Blend until smooth and creamy. For a thicker consistency, add a few ice cubes and blend again.

Pour the smoothie mixture into serving bowls.

Garnish the smoothie bowls with your favorite low-carb toppings, such as sliced almonds, extra chia seeds or additional berries.

Serve immediately and enjoy the refreshing and satisfying Berry Bliss Low-Carb Smoothie Bowl!

Nutritional Values (per serving): Calories 250 | Fat 12g | Carbohydrates 18g | Protein 20g

3. Spinach-Feta Omelette Roll-Ups

Preparation Time: 10 minutes | Cooking Time: 15 minutes | Servings: 2

Ingredients:

- Fresh spinach, chopped: 5 cups
- Feta cheese, crumbled: 1/2 cup
- Eggs: 4 large
- Cream cheese: 2 tablespoons
- Olive oil: 1 tablespoon
- Dried oregano: 1 teaspoon
- Salt and pepper: to taste

- Instructions:

Heat olive oil in a pan over medium heat.

Add the chopped spinach and sauté until wilted, about 3-4 minutes.

In a bowl, mix the sautéed spinach with the crumbled feta cheese. Set aside.

Crack the eggs into a mixing bowl.

Add cream cheese, dried oregano, salt and pepper. Whisk until well combined.

Heat a non-stick pan over medium heat.

Pour half of the omelette batter into the pan, swirling to evenly distribute.

Cook for 2-3 minutes until the edges firm up, then flip and cook for another 1-2 minutes.

Repeat the process with the remaining batter.

Place each omelette on a flat surface.

Evenly spread half of the spinach-feta filling over each omelette.

Carefully roll each omelette into a tight cylinder.

With a sharp knife, cut each rolled omelette into bite-sized rolls.

Arrange the roll-ups on a plate and serve immediately.

Nutritional Values (per serving): Calories 320 | Fat 25g | Carbohydrates 6g | Protein 18g

4. Keto-Friendly Chia Seed Pudding

Preparation Time: 10 minutes | Cooking Time: 0 minutes | Servings: 2-4

Ingredients:

- Chia seeds: 1/4 cup
- Unsweetened almond milk: 1 2/3 cups
- Unsweetened cocoa powder: 1 tablespoon
- Vanilla extract: 1 teaspoon
- Erythritol (or preferred low-carb sweetener): 2 tablespoons
- Fresh berries (for topping): 1/3 cup

Instructions:

In a mixing bowl, combine chia seeds, unsweetened almond milk, cocoa powder, vanilla extract and erythritol.

Stir the mixture thoroughly, ensuring the chia seeds are evenly distributed.

Let the mixture sit for 5 minutes, stirring occasionally to prevent clumping.

After 5 minutes, cover the bowl and refrigerate for at least 2 hours or overnight, allowing the chia seeds to absorb the liquid and create a pudding-like consistency.

Before serving, stir the mixture one last time to break up any clumps.

Spoon the chia seed pudding into individual serving bowls.

Garnish each serving with fresh berries.

Nutritional Values (per serving): Calories 180 | Fat 10g | Carbohydrates 15g | Protein 5g

5. Quick and Easy Bacon Egg Muffins

Preparation Time: 10 minutes | Cooking Time: 20 minutes | Servings: 2

Ingredients:

- Bacon, diced: 1 cup
- Cherry tomatoes, halved: 1 cup
- Bell pepper, diced: 1/2 cup
- Eggs: 4 large
- Cheddar cheese, grated: 1/4 cup
- Salt and pepper: to taste
- Fresh chives, chopped (for garnishing)

Instructions:

Preheat the oven to 180°C (350°F).

Grease a muffin tin or line with paper liners.

Cook the bacon dice in a pan over medium heat until crispy. Remove excess fat.

Add cherry tomatoes and bell pepper to the same pan. Sauté until the vegetables are slightly softened.

Evenly distribute the cooked bacon and vegetable mixture among the muffin cups.

Crack the Eggs:

Carefully crack an egg into each muffin cup over the bacon and vegetables.

Season with salt and pepper to taste. Sprinkle grated Cheddar cheese on top.

Place the muffin tin in the preheated oven and bake for about 15-20 minutes, until the egg whites are set.

Remove from the oven and let cool for a few minutes. Garnish with fresh chives before serving.

Nutritional Values (per serving): Calories 320 | Fat 24g | Carbohydrates 4g | Protein 21g

6. Greek Yogurt Parfait with Nuts and Berries

Preparation Time: 10 minutes | Cooking Time: 0 minutes | Servings: 2

Ingredients:

- Greek yogurt: 1 2/3 cups
- Mixed nuts (almonds, walnuts, pistachios), chopped: 2/3 cup
- Mixed berries (strawberries, blueberries, raspberries): 1 cup
- Chia seeds: 1 1/2 tablespoons
- Unsweetened shredded coconut: 2 tablespoons
- Vanilla extract: 1 teaspoon
- Sugar-free sweetener (optional): 1 tablespoon
- Fresh mint leaves: for garnishing

Instructions:

In a bowl, mix Greek yogurt and vanilla extract. If desired, add a sugar-free sweetener for additional sweetness. Mix well.

Layer the parfait in glasses or bowls. Start with a spoonful of the Greek yogurt mixture at the bottom.

Add a layer of mixed nuts, followed by a layer of mixed berries.

Sprinkle a portion of chia seeds over the berries, then add another layer of the Greek yogurt mixture.

Continue layering until you reach the top, finishing with a sprinkle of shredded coconut.

Garnish each parfait with fresh mint leaves to enhance the flavor.

Serve immediately and enjoy this delicious Greek Yogurt Parfait with Nuts and Berries.

Nutritional Values (per serving): Calories 350 | Fat 18g | Carbohydrates 25g | Protein 20g

7. Zucchini and Cheese Breakfast Casserole

Preparation Time: 15 minutes | Cooking Time: 35 minutes | Servings: 4

Ingredients:
- Zucchini, grated: 4 cups
- Cheddar cheese, grated: 2 cups
- Mozzarella cheese, grated: 1 1/2 cups
- Eggs: 8 large
- Cooked and crumbled bacon: 1 1/2 cups
- Almond flour: 1 cup
- Sour cream: 2/3 cup
- Unsalted butter, melted: 1/4 cup
- Baking powder: 1 teaspoon
- Garlic powder: 1 teaspoon
- Salt and pepper: to taste
- Fresh chives, chopped (for garnishing)

Instructions:
Preheat the oven to 180°C (350°F). Grease a casserole dish with butter or cooking spray.

In a large bowl, mix together the grated zucchini, Cheddar cheese, Mozzarella cheese and fried bacon.

In a separate bowl, whisk together the eggs, almond flour, sour cream, melted butter, baking powder, garlic powder, salt and pepper until well combined.

Pour the egg mixture over the zucchini and cheese mixture. Stir everything until evenly mixed.

Transfer the mixture to the prepared casserole dish and spread it evenly.

Bake in the preheated oven for 35 minutes, until the top is golden brown and the center is set.

Remove from the oven and let it cool for a few minutes before slicing.

Garnish with fresh chopped chives before serving.

Nutritional Values (per serving): Calories 480 | Fat 38g | Carbohydrates 8g | Protein 25g

8. Almond Flour Pancakes with Sugar-Free Syrup

Preparation Time: 10 minutes | Cooking Time: 15 minutes | Servings: 4

Ingredients:
- Almond flour: 2 cups
- Eggs: 4 large

- Unsweetened almond milk: 1 cup
- Baking powder: 1 teaspoon
- Vanilla extract: 1/2 teaspoon
- Salt: 1/4 teaspoon
- Butter or oil: for cooking

Sugar-Free Syrup:
- Water: 1/2 cup
- Erythritol (or your preferred sugar substitute): 1 cup
- Vanilla extract: 1 teaspoon
- Salt: a pinch

Instructions:

In a mixing bowl, whisk together almond flour, eggs, almond milk, baking powder, vanilla extract and salt until well combined.

Heat a non-stick pan or griddle over medium heat. Add a little butter or oil for frying.

Pour about 60ml of the batter into the pan for each pancake. Cook until bubbles form on the surface, then flip and cook until the other side is golden brown.

Repeat the process until all the batter is used, adding more butter or oil to the pan as needed.

Sugar-free syrup: in a small saucepan, combine water, Erythritol, vanilla extract and a pinch of salt. Bring to a simmer over medium heat.

Stir until the Erythritol is completely dissolved and the syrup slightly thickens.

Remove from heat and let cool for a few minutes before serving.

Nutritional Values (per serving): Calories 280 | Fat 22g | Carbohydrates 8g | Protein 12g

9. Green Goddess Keto Smoothie

Preparation Time: 5 minutes | Cooking Time: 0 minutes | Servings: 2

Ingredients:
- Fresh spinach: 5 cups
- Avocado, peeled and pitted: 1/2 medium
- Cucumber, diced: 3/4 cup
- Fresh mint leaves: 1/2 cup
- Unsweetened almond milk: 1 cup
- Chia seeds: 1 tablespoon
- Ice cubes: (optional)

Instructions:
Place fresh spinach, avocado, cucumber and mint leaves into a blender.

Add the unsweetened almond milk to the blender.

Blend the ingredients until smooth and creamy.

If you prefer a cooler smoothie, add ice cubes and blend again until everything is well mixed.

Once the smoothie has reached the desired consistency, add the chia seeds and pulse briefly to mix them evenly.

Pour the Green Goddess Keto Smoothie into glasses and serve immediately.

Nutritional Values (per serving): Calories 180 | Fat 12g | Carbohydrates 10g | Protein 5g

10. Avocado Stuffed with Smoked Salmon and Cream Cheese

Preparation Time: 10 minutes | Cooking Time: 0 minutes | Servings: 2

Ingredients:
- Ripe avocados: 2 medium (approx. 14 oz)
- Smoked salmon, thinly sliced: 3.5 oz
- Cream cheese: 2/3 cup
- Fresh dill, chopped: 1 tablespoon
- Capers, drained: 1 tablespoon
- Lemon juice: 1 teaspoon
- Salt and pepper: to taste

Instructions:
Halve the avocados and remove the pits. Scoop out a small amount of flesh from the center with a spoon to create a larger well for the filling.

In a bowl, mix together cream cheese, smoked salmon, fresh dill, capers and lemon juice. Stir well until all ingredients are evenly incorporated.

Season the mixture with salt and pepper. Remember that smoked salmon and capers already contribute some saltiness, so be cautious with additional salt.

Spoon the cream cheese-smoked salmon mixture into the wells of the halved avocados, distributing it evenly.

Garnish with a bit of dill and a few extra capers.

Serve immediately and enjoy this quick and delicious low-carb dish!

Nutritional Values (per serving): Calories 420 | Fat 38g | Carbohydrates 9g | Protein 12g

11. Turmeric Scrambled Eggs with Sautéed Spinach

Preparation Time: 10 minutes | Cooking Time: 10 minutes | Servings: 2

Ingredients:
- Eggs: 4 large (approx. 8.5 oz)
- Fresh spinach, chopped: 5 cups
- Olive oil: 1 tablespoon (0.5 oz)
- Ground turmeric: 1/2 teaspoon (0.03 oz)
- Salt and pepper: to taste

Instructions:

Crack the eggs into a bowl and whisk until well blended.

Chop the fresh spinach.

Heat olive oil in a non-stick pan over medium heat.

Add the chopped spinach and sauté for about 2-3 minutes until wilted.

Sprinkle ground turmeric over the sautéed spinach and stir.

Pour the whisked eggs into the pan with spinach and turmeric.

Stir continuously until the eggs are scrambled and cooked to your liking, about 3-4 minutes.

Season the scrambled eggs with salt and pepper.

Remove from heat and serve immediately.

Nutritional Values (per serving): Calories 320 | Fat 24g | Carbohydrates 5g | Protein 21g

12. Cauliflower Hash Browns with Avocado Dip

Preparation Time: 15 minutes | Cooking Time: 20 minutes | Servings: 4

Ingredients:
- Cauliflower, grated: 4 cups

- Eggs: 2 large
- Almond flour: 1/2 cup
- Parmesan cheese, grated: 1/2 cup
- Garlic powder: 1 teaspoon
- Onion powder: 1 teaspoon
- Salt and pepper: to taste
- Olive oil: 2 tablespoons

Avocado Dip:
- Ripe avocados: 2 medium
- Garlic, chopped: 1 clove
- Lime juice: from 1 lime
- Salt and pepper: to taste

Instructions:
Preheat the oven to 200°C (400°F).

In a large bowl, mix together grated cauliflower, eggs, almond flour, Parmesan cheese, garlic powder, onion powder, salt and pepper. Mix well until all ingredients are evenly incorporated.

Form the cauliflower mixture into hash browns and place them on a baking sheet lined with parchment paper.

Brush the hash browns with olive oil to ensure they become golden and crispy.

Bake in the preheated oven for 15-20 minutes, until the edges are golden brown and crispy.

While the hash browns are baking, prepare the avocado dip. Mash the ripe avocados in a bowl and mix with chopped garlic, lime juice, salt and pepper.

Once the cauliflower is done, remove it from the oven and let it cool for a few minutes.

Serve the cauliflower hash browns with the avocado dip on the side.

Nutritional Values (per serving): Calories 220 | Fat 15g | Carbohydrates 12g | Protein 8g

13. Low-Carb Blueberry Almond Muffins

Preparation Time: 15 minutes | Cooking Time: 20 minutes | Servings: 4

Ingredients:

- Almond flour: 1 1/2 cups
- Coconut flour: 1/2 cup
- Baking powder: 1 teaspoon
- Baking soda: 1/2 teaspoon
- Salt: 1/4 teaspoon
- Eggs: 2 large
- Unsweetened almond milk: 1/2 cup
- Melted coconut oil: 1/4 cup
- Granulated sweetener (Stevia or Erythritol): 1/4 cup
- Vanilla extract: 1 teaspoon
- Fresh blueberries: 1 cup

Instructions:

Preheat the oven to 180°C and line a muffin tin with paper liners.

In a large bowl, whisk together almond flour, coconut flour, baking powder, baking soda and salt.

In a separate bowl, whisk the eggs, then add almond milk, melted coconut oil, sweetener and vanilla extract. Stir until well combined.

Add the wet ingredients to the dry ingredients and stir until just combined. Be careful not to overmix.

Gently fold in the fresh blueberries.

Spoon the batter into the muffin cups, filling each about two-thirds full.

Bake in the preheated oven for 18-20 minutes or until a toothpick inserted into the center comes out clean.

Allow the muffins to cool in the tin for 5 minutes, then transfer them to a wire rack to cool completely.

Nutritional Values (per serving): Calories 220 | Fat 18g | Carbohydrates 8g | Protein 6g

14. Coconut Chia Seed Pudding with Lime Zest

Preparation Time: 10 minutes | Cooking Time: 0 minutes | Servings: 2

Ingredients:

- Chia seeds: 1/4 cup

- Unsweetened coconut milk: 1 2/3 cups
- Shredded coconut: 1/4 cup
- Low-carb sweetener (e.g., Erythritol): 1 tablespoon
- Vanilla extract: 1 teaspoon
- Zest of 1 lime
- Salt: a pinch

Instructions:

In a mixing bowl, combine chia seeds, coconut milk, shredded coconut, low-carb sweetener, vanilla extract, lime zest and a pinch of salt.

Stir the mixture well to evenly distribute the ingredients. Let it sit for 5 minutes.

After 5 minutes, stir the mixture again to prevent clumping. Cover the bowl and refrigerate for at least 4 hours or overnight.

Once the pudding has set, stir it well again. If it's too thick, add a little more coconut milk to achieve the desired consistency.

Serve the coconut chia seed pudding in individual bowls or glasses.

Nutritional Values (per serving): Calories 250 | Fat 18g | Carbohydrates 12g | Protein 6g

15.   Ham and Cheese Egg Muffins

Preparation Time: 15 minutes | Cooking Time: 20 minutes | Servings: 4

Ingredients:
- Broccoli, finely chopped: 2 1/2 cups
- Cooked ham, diced: 1 cup
- Cheddar cheese, grated: 1 1/2 cups
- Eggs: 8 large
- Heavy cream: 1/2 cup
- Olive oil: 1 teaspoon
- Garlic powder: 1/2 teaspoon
- Onion powder: 1/2 teaspoon
- Salt and pepper: to taste

Instructions:

Preheat the oven to 180°C (350°F) and grease a muffin tin with olive oil.

Sauté the chopped broccoli in a pan over medium heat until it's soft. Add the diced ham and sauté until slightly browned.

In a bowl, whisk together eggs, heavy cream, garlic powder, onion powder, salt and pepper.

Distribute the sautéed broccoli and ham evenly among the muffin cups.

Pour the egg mixture over the broccoli and ham in each cup, filling almost to the top.

Sprinkle grated Cheddar cheese over each muffin cup.

Bake in the preheated oven for 20 minutes or until the muffins are set and the top is golden brown.

Allow the muffins to cool for a few minutes before carefully removing them from the muffin tin.

Nutritional Values (per serving): Calories 320 | Fat 24g | Carbohydrates 4g | Protein 21g

16. Creamy Keto Coffee Smoothie

Preparation Time: 5 minutes | Cooking Time: 0 minutes | Servings: 2

Ingredients:
- Brewed and chilled coffee: 1 cup
- Unsweetened almond milk: 3/4 cup
- Ice cubes: 1 cup
- MCT oil: 2 tablespoons
- Unsweetened cocoa powder: 2 tablespoons
- Chia seeds: 1 tablespoon
- Erythritol (or any keto-friendly sweetener): 1 teaspoon
- Vanilla extract: 1/2 teaspoon
- Salt: a pinch

Instructions:

Place the chilled coffee, almond milk, ice cubes, MCT oil, cocoa powder, chia seeds, Erythritol, vanilla extract and a pinch of salt into a blender.

Blend on high until all ingredients are well mixed and the mixture is smooth and creamy.

Taste the smoothie and adjust the sweetness if necessary by adding more Erythritol.

Pour the creamy keto coffee smoothie into glasses and serve immediately.

Nutritional Values (per serving): Calories 120 | Fat 10g | Carbohydrates 5g | Protein 2g

17. Mushroom and Swiss Cheese Frittata

Preparation Time: 15 minutes | Cooking Time: 20 minutes | Servings: 4

Ingredients:
- Mushrooms, sliced: 2 1/2 cups
- Swiss cheese, grated: 1 1/2 cups
- Eggs: 8 large
- Heavy cream: 1/2 cup
- Small onion, finely diced: 1/2 cup
- Garlic, chopped: 2 cloves
- Butter: 2 tablespoons
- Salt and pepper: to taste
- Fresh parsley: for garnishing

Instructions:

Preheat the oven to 180°C (350°F).

In a large oven-proof skillet, melt the butter over medium heat. Add the chopped onions and sauté until translucent.

Add the sliced mushrooms to the pan and cook until they release their moisture and turn golden brown.

Stir in the chopped garlic and cook for another minute until fragrant.

In a bowl, whisk together the eggs, heavy cream, salt and pepper.

Pour the egg mixture over the mushrooms and onions in the skillet. Let it cook undisturbed for a few minutes, until the edges start to set.

Sprinkle the grated Swiss cheese evenly over the frittata.

Transfer the skillet to the preheated oven and bake for about 15-20 minutes, until the frittata is set in the middle and the cheese is melted and bubbly.

Remove from the oven and let it cool for a few minutes before slicing.

Garnish with fresh parsley and serve hot.

Nutritional Values (per serving): Calories 320 | Fat 25g | Carbohydrates 4g | Protein 18g

18. Breakfast Wrap with Avocado and Bacon

Preparation Time: 10 minutes | Cooking Time: 15 minutes | Servings: 2

Ingredients:

- Eggs: 4 large (approx. 8.5 oz)
- Bacon, crisply fried: 4 slices (approx. 4.2 oz)
- Ripe avocado, sliced: 1 medium (approx. 7 oz)
- Low-carb tortillas: 4 (approx. 5.6 oz)
- Shredded Cheddar cheese: 1/2 cup
- Salt and pepper: to taste
- Fresh cilantro: for garnishing

Instructions:

In a non-stick pan over medium heat, fry the bacon slices until crispy. Remove from the pan and let them drain on paper towels. Crumble the bacon into small pieces.

In the same pan, using the bacon fat, crack the eggs and fry them to your desired doneness. Season with salt and pepper.

Warm the low-carb tortillas in the pan for about 10 seconds on each side.

Assemble the wraps by placing a warmed tortilla on a plate. Add a layer of sliced avocado, then the fried eggs, crumbled bacon and shredded Cheddar cheese.

Fold the sides of the tortilla toward the center and roll it up tightly to form a wrap.

Repeat the process for the remaining tortillas.

Garnish with fresh cilantro and serve immediately.

Nutritional Values (per serving): Calories 480 | Fat 32g | Carbohydrates 22g | Protein 24g

19. Vanilla Almond Butter Keto Porridge

Preparation Time: 15 minutes | Cooking Time: 10 minutes | Servings: 2

Ingredients:
- Almond flour: 1 cup
- Coconut flour: 1/4 cup
- Chia seeds: 2 tablespoons
- Almond butter: 1/4 cup
- Unsweetened almond milk: 2 cups
- Vanilla extract: 1 teaspoon
- Cinnamon: 1/2 teaspoon
- Salt: a pinch
- Low-carb sweetener: to taste
- Sliced almonds and fresh berries: for garnishing (optional)

Instructions:

In a medium-sized saucepan, combine almond flour, coconut flour, chia seeds, almond butter and almond milk.

Place the saucepan over medium heat and stir continuously to prevent clumping. Cook for about 8-10 minutes until the mixture reaches your desired consistency.

Stir in vanilla extract, cinnamon, salt and sweetener to taste.

Once the porridge has reached the desired consistency, remove from heat and let it cool for a minute.

Distribute the porridge into serving bowls and garnish with sliced almonds and fresh berries if desired.

Nutritional Values (per serving): Calories 420 | Fat 34g | Carbohydrates 15g | Protein 15g

20. Sausage Vegetable Scramble

Preparation Time: 10 minutes | Cooking Time: 15 minutes | Servings: 4

Ingredients:
- Pork sausage, crumbled: 14 oz
- Bell peppers, diced (mixed colors): 1 1/2 cups
- Zucchini, diced: 1 1/2 cups
- Cherry tomatoes, halved: 1 cup

- Red onions, finely chopped: 2/3 cup
- Eggs: 4 large
- Cheddar cheese, grated: 1/2 cup
- Olive oil: 2 tablespoons
- Salt and pepper: to taste
- Fresh parsley, chopped: for garnishing

Instructions:

Heat olive oil in a large pan over medium heat.

Add the crumbled pork sausage and cook until browned and cooked through.

Add the chopped red onion to the pan and sauté until translucent.

Stir in the diced bell peppers and zucchini. Continue cooking for another 5-7 minutes until the vegetables soften.

Add the cherry tomatoes to the pan and cook briefly until they begin to soften.

Push the sausage-vegetable mixture to one side of the pan to make space for the eggs.

Crack the eggs into the empty side of the pan. Gently scramble the eggs until fully cooked.

Once the eggs are cooked, mix them into the sausage-vegetable mixture.

Sprinkle the grated Cheddar cheese over the top and stir until the cheese is melted and everything is well combined.

Season with salt and pepper to taste.

Garnish with chopped fresh parsley.

Nutritional Values (per serving): Calories 450 | Fat 35g | Carbohydrates 8g | Protein 24g

Chapter 5: Lunch

21.   Spicy Chicken Caesar Salad

Preparation Time: 15 minutes | Cooking Time: 15 minutes | Servings: 2-4

Ingredients:

- Boneless, skinless chicken breast, grilled and sliced: 10.5 oz
- Romaine lettuce, washed and chopped: 4 cups
- Parmesan cheese, shaved: 1/2 cup
- Cherry tomatoes, halved: 1/4 cup
- Black olives, sliced: 1/4 cup
- Caesar dressing: 1/4 cup
- Olive oil: 1 tablespoon (0.5 oz)
- Garlic clove, chopped: 1 clove
- Dijon mustard: 1 teaspoon
- Worcestershire sauce: 1 teaspoon
- Salt and pepper: to taste

Instructions:

For the dressing, in a small bowl whisk together olive oil, chopped garlic, Dijon mustard, Worcestershire sauce, salt and pepper.

Grill the chicken breasts until fully cooked, then slice them into thin strips.

In a large bowl, mix together the chopped Romaine lettuce, cherry tomatoes, black olives and Parmesan cheese.

Add the grilled and sliced chicken to the bowl.

Pour the Caesar dressing over the salad and toss until all ingredients are well coated.

Divide the salad into individual portions and serve on plates.

Serve immediately and enjoy this spicy, low-carb Chicken Caesar Salad, perfect for busy individuals.

Nutritional Values (per serving): Calories 320 | Fat 18g | Carbohydrates 7g | Protein 32g

22.   Stuffed Chicken Wraps with Mushrooms and Spinach

Preparation Time: 20 minutes | Cooking Time: 25 minutes | Servings: 4

Ingredients:
- Boneless, skinless chicken breasts: 1.3 lbs
- Fresh spinach, chopped: 7 cups
- Mushrooms, finely diced: 1 1/2 cups
- Cream cheese: 1/2 cup
- Grated Parmesan cheese: 1/2 cup
- Garlic, chopped: 2 cloves
- Olive oil: 1 tablespoon
- Dried oregano: 1 teaspoon
- Paprika: 1 teaspoon
- Salt and pepper: to taste
- Large lettuce leaves (for wrapping): 8 leaves

Instructions:

Preheat your oven to 200°C (392°F) or 180°C (356°F) for fan-assisted.

Place the chicken breasts flat on a cutting board. Carefully slice each breast horizontally to create a pocket, but do not cut all the way through.

In a pan, heat olive oil over medium heat. Add chopped garlic and diced mushrooms and sauté until the mushrooms are soft. Add chopped spinach and continue to cook until wilted. Remove from heat and let it cool.

In a bowl, mix the sautéed vegetables, cream cheese, Parmesan cheese, dried oregano, paprika, salt and pepper.

Carefully fill each chicken breast pocket with the mushroom and spinach mixture.

Seal and Bake: Secure the openings of the chicken pockets with toothpicks. Place the stuffed chicken on a baking tray and bake in the preheated oven for 20-25 minutes, until the chicken is cooked through.

After baking, remove the toothpicks and slice the stuffed chicken into strips. Place each strip on a lettuce leaf and roll up, securing with toothpicks if needed.

Arrange the wraps on a plate and serve immediately.

Nutritional Values (per serving): Calories 380 | Fat 18g | Carbohydrates 6g | Protein 45g

23.   Creamy Broccoli Cheddar Soup

Preparation Time: 15 minutes | Cooking Time: 25 minutes | Servings: 4

Ingredients:

- Broccoli, chopped: 4 cups
- Cheddar cheese, grated: 2 cups
- Onion, diced: 1 cup
- Garlic, chopped: 2 cloves
- Unsalted butter: 1/4 cup
- Almond flour: 1/4 cup
- Vegetable broth: 4 cups
- Heavy cream: 1 cup
- Salt and pepper: to taste
- Nutmeg, freshly grated: 1 teaspoon

Instructions:

In a large pot, melt the butter over medium heat. Add diced onions and chopped garlic. Sauté until the onions are translucent.

Sprinkle almond flour over the onion-garlic mixture. Stir constantly and cook for about 2-3 minutes to make a roux.

Gradually add the vegetable broth while stirring continuously to prevent lumps. Bring the mixture to a simmer.

Add the chopped broccoli to the pot. Cook for about 10-12 minutes until the broccoli is soft.

Use an immersion blender to purée the soup until smooth. If you prefer a chunkier texture, blend it to your desired consistency.

Reduce the heat to low and stir in the heavy cream, grated Cheddar cheese and grated nutmeg. Continue stirring until the cheese is melted and the soup is creamy.

Season with salt and pepper. Adjust the consistency if necessary with additional broth or cream.

Once everything is well mixed and heated through, remove the soup from the heat.

Nutritional Values (per serving): Calories 350 | Fat 28g | Carbohydrates 10g | Protein 15g

24. Grilled Shrimp and Avocado Salad with Lime Vinaigrette

Preparation Time: 15 minutes | Cooking Time: 10 minutes | Servings: 4

Ingredients:

- Large shrimp, peeled and deveined: 1.1 lbs
- Ripe avocados, diced: 2 medium
- Cherry tomatoes, halved: 1 1/2 cups
- Mixed salad greens: 4 cups
- Red onion, thinly sliced: 1/2 cup
- Fresh cilantro, chopped: 1/4 cup
For the Lime Vinaigrette:
- Olive oil: 3 tablespoons
- Fresh lime juice: 2 tablespoons
- Garlic, chopped: 1 clove
- Dijon mustard: 1 teaspoon
- Salt and pepper: to taste

Instructions:

Preheat the grill to medium-high heat.

In a bowl, toss the shrimp with a splash of olive oil, salt and pepper. Thread onto skewers.

Grill the shrimp for 2-3 minutes per side, until opaque and cooked through.

In a large salad bowl, mix the diced avocados, cherry tomatoes, mixed salad greens, sliced red onion and chopped cilantro.

In a small bowl, whisk together olive oil, lime juice, chopped garlic, Dijon mustard, salt and pepper to create the lime vinaigrette.

Drizzle the lime vinaigrette over the salad and gently toss to coat.

Remove the grilled shrimp from the skewers and arrange them on top of the salad.

Serve immediately and enjoy a refreshing and flavorful low-carb meal!

Nutritional Values (per serving): Calories 350 | Fat 22g | Carbohydrates 12g | Protein 28g

25. Turkey and Vegetable Salad Wraps

Preparation Time: 15 minutes | Cooking Time: 15 minutes | Servings: 2

Ingredients:

- Ground turkey: 1.1 lbs
- Mushrooms, finely chopped: 2 1/2 cups
- Bell peppers, diced: 1 cup
- Carrots, julienned: 1 cup
- Green onions, chopped: 1/2 cup
- Garlic, chopped: 2 cloves
- Soy sauce: 2 tablespoons
- Sesame oil: 1 tablespoon
- Olive oil: 2 teaspoons
- Ginger, grated: 1 tablespoon
- Salt and pepper: to taste
- Iceberg lettuce, leaves separated: 1 head

Instructions:

In a large pan over medium heat, brown the ground turkey in olive oil. Cook until the turkey is browned and fully cooked, breaking it up with a spoon.

Add the chopped garlic and grated ginger to the skillet. Sauté for 2 minutes until fragrant.

Stir in the mushrooms, bell peppers, carrots and green onions. Cook for another 5-7 minutes until the vegetables are soft.

Pour the soy sauce and sesame oil over the turkey and vegetable mixture. Stir well to combine. Season with salt and pepper to taste.

Carefully separate individual leaves from the head of iceberg lettuce to create shells for the filling.

Evenly spoon the turkey-vegetable mixture into each lettuce cup.

Nutritional Values (per serving): Calories 320 | Fat 18g | Carbohydrates 10g | Protein 28g

26. Cauliflower Bacon Chowder

Preparation Time: 15 minutes | Cooking Time: 25 minutes | Servings: 2

Ingredients:
- Cauliflower, chopped: 4 cups
- Bacon, diced: 7 oz
- Leek, sliced: 1 1/2 cups
- Celery, diced: 1 cup
- Garlic, chopped: 2 cloves
- Butter: 2 tablespoons
- Chicken broth: 4 cups
- Heavy cream: 1 cup
- Dried thyme: 1 teaspoon
- Salt and pepper: to taste
- Cheddar cheese, grated (for garnishing): 1/2 cup
- Fresh chives, chopped (for garnishing)

Instructions:
In a large pot, melt the butter over medium heat. Add the diced bacon and fry until crispy. Remove half of the bacon for garnishing later.

Add the leek, celery and chopped garlic to the pot. Sauté until the vegetables are soft.

Pour in the chicken broth and add the chopped cauliflower. Bring to a boil, then reduce heat and simmer until the cauliflower is soft.

Purée the soup with an immersion blender until smooth. If you don't have an immersion blender, transfer the mixture in batches to a blender and then return it to the pot.

Stir in the heavy cream and dried thyme. Season with salt and pepper to taste.

Simmer for another 5-10 minutes to blend the flavors.

Ladle the soup into bowls. Garnish each serving with the reserved crispy bacon, grated Cheddar cheese and chopped fresh chives.

Nutritional Values (per serving): Calories 350 | Fat 28g | Carbohydrates 10g | Protein 12g

27. Mediterranean Quinoa Salad with Feta and Olives

Preparation Time: 15 minutes | Cooking Time: 15 minutes | Servings: 4

Ingredients:

- Quinoa: 1 cup
- Water: 1 2/3 cups
- Cherry tomatoes, halved: 1 cup
- Cucumber, diced: 3/4 cup
- Kalamata olives, pitted and sliced: 1/2 cup
- Feta cheese, crumbled: 1 cup
- Red onions, finely chopped: 1/3 cup
- Fresh parsley, chopped: 1/4 cup
- Extra virgin olive oil: 2 tablespoons
- Red wine vinegar: 1 tablespoon
- Dried oregano: 1 teaspoon
- Salt and pepper: to taste

Instructions:

Rinse the quinoa under cold water. Combine quinoa and water in a medium-sized saucepan. Bring to a boil, then reduce heat and simmer covered for 15 minutes, until quinoa is cooked and water is absorbed. Fluff with a fork and let cool.

In a large bowl, mix the cooked quinoa, cherry tomatoes, cucumbers, Kalamata olives, feta cheese, red onions and fresh parsley.

In a small bowl, whisk together olive oil, red wine vinegar, dried oregano, salt and pepper. Pour the dressing over the quinoa mixture and gently stir to ensure all ingredients are well coated.

Refrigerate the salad for at least 30 minutes before serving to allow the flavors to meld.

Nutritional Values (per serving): Calories 350 | Fat 18g | Carbohydrates 35g | Protein 12g

28. Spicy Chicken and Roasted Vegetables

Preparation Time: 15 minutes | Cooking Time: 20 minutes | Servings: 4

Ingredients:

- Boneless, skinless chicken breast, thinly sliced: 1.1 lbs
- Broccoli florets: 4 cups
- Bell peppers, thinly sliced (mix of red, yellow, and green): 1 1/2 cups
- Sugar snap peas, ends trimmed: 1 cup
- Green onions, sliced: 1/2 cup
- Garlic, chopped: 2 cloves
- Fresh ginger, chopped: 1 tablespoon
- Soy sauce: 3 tablespoons
- Sesame oil: 2 tablespoons
- Chili garlic sauce: 1 tablespoon (adjust to taste)
- Olive oil: 1 tablespoon
- Erythritol (or preferred low-carb sweetener): 1 teaspoon
- Salt and pepper: to taste
- Sesame seeds: for garnishing

Instructions:

Slice the chicken into thin strips.

Cut broccoli into small florets.

Slice the bell peppers thinly.

Trim the sugar snap peas and slice the green onions.

Chop the garlic and ginger.

In a bowl, stir together soy sauce, chili garlic sauce and Erythritol.

Add the sliced chicken to the marinade and let sit for at least 10 minutes.

Heat olive oil in a wok or large frying pan over medium-high heat.

Add the marinated chicken and stir-fry until cooked through. Remove from the wok and set aside.

Add sesame oil to the same wok.

Stir-fry garlic and ginger until fragrant.

Add broccoli, bell peppers and sugar snap peas. Cook until the vegetables are crisp-tender.

Return the cooked chicken to the wok.

Pour the remaining marinade over and mix everything together.

Season with salt and pepper to taste.

Stir in the sliced green onions.

Garnish with sesame seeds.

Serve hot.

Nutritional Values (per serving): Calories 350 | Fat 15g | Carbohydrates 10g | Protein 40g

29.   Tomato Basil Zoodle Salad

Preparation Time: 15 minutes | Cooking Time: 0 minutes | Servings: 2

Ingredients:
- Zucchini, spiralized into zoodles: 4 cups
- Cherry tomatoes, halved: 1 1/2 cups
- Fresh basil leaves, chopped: 1/2 cup
- Pine nuts, toasted: 1/4 cup
- Parmesan cheese, shaved: 1/4 cup
- Cold-pressed olive oil: 2 tablespoons
- Balsamic vinegar: 1 tablespoon
- Salt and pepper: to taste

Instructions:

In a large bowl, mix together the zucchini zoodles, cherry tomatoes, fresh basil, toasted pine nuts and Parmesan.

In a small bowl, whisk together the cold-pressed olive oil and balsamic vinegar to prepare the dressing. Season with salt and pepper to taste.

Pour the dressing over the noodle mixture and gently toss until all ingredients are well coated.

Allow the salad to sit for at least 10 minutes to let the flavors meld.

Serve the Tomato Basil Zoodle Salad in individual portions, garnished with additional Parmesan and fresh basil if desired.

Nutritional Values (per serving): Calories 280 | Fat 22g | Carbohydrates 10g | Protein 8g

30. Lemon Garlic Chicken Thighs with Asparagus One-Pot

Preparation Time: 10 minutes | Cooking Time: 30 minutes | Servings: 4

Ingredients:

- Chicken thighs, bone-in and skin-on: 1.3 lbs
- Fresh asparagus, trimmed: 4 cups
- Lemon, sliced: 1
- Garlic, chopped: 4 cloves
- Unsalted butter: 3 1/2 tablespoons
- Olive oil: 2 tablespoons
- Dried thyme: 1 teaspoon
- Salt and black pepper: to taste
- Fresh parsley: for garnishing

Instructions:

Preheat the oven to 200°C (392°F) or 180°C (356°F) for fan-assisted.

Season the chicken thighs with salt, black pepper and dried thyme.

Heat olive oil in a large oven-safe skillet over medium-high heat. Add the chicken thighs skin-side down and sear until golden brown, about 3-4 minutes per side.

Remove the chicken from the skillet and set aside.

Add the chopped garlic to the same skillet and sauté until fragrant.

Return the chicken to the skillet, add the asparagus spears and place lemon slices between the chicken pieces.

Brush the chicken and asparagus with butter and transfer the skillet to the preheated oven.

Bake for 20-25 minutes or until the chicken reaches an internal temperature of 75°C (167°F).

Garnish with fresh parsley before serving.

Nutritional Values (per serving): Calories 480 | Fat 32g | Carbohydrates 8g | Protein 40g

31. Kale Avocado Salad with Lemon Dijon Dressing

Preparation Time: 15 minutes | Cooking Time: 0 minutes | Servings: 4

Ingredients:

- Fresh kale, stems removed and chopped: 4 cups
- Ripe avocados, diced: 1 medium (approx. 7 oz)
- Cherry tomatoes, halved: 1/2 cup
- Cucumber, thinly sliced: 1/2 cup
- Red onion, thinly sliced: 1/4 cup
- Feta cheese, crumbled: 1/4 cup
For the Lemon Dijon Dressing:
- Olive oil: 1/4 cup
- Lemon juice: 2 tablespoons
- Dijon mustard: 2 teaspoons
- Garlic, chopped: 1 clove
- Salt and pepper: to taste

Instructions:

In a large bowl, mix together the chopped kale, diced avocados, cherry tomatoes, cucumber, red onion and crumbled feta cheese.

In a small bowl, whisk together the olive oil, lemon juice, Dijon mustard, chopped garlic, salt and pepper to create the lemon Dijon dressing.

Pour the dressing over the salad and gently toss to ensure all ingredients are well coated.

Allow the salad to sit for at least 10 minutes to let the flavors meld.

Serve the salad in individual portions, ensuring a good distribution of ingredients in each serving.

Nutritional Values (per serving): Calories 280 | Fat 21g | Carbohydrates 15g | Protein 7g

32. Cabbage and Sausage Skillet

Preparation Time: 15 minutes | Cooking Time: 25 minutes | Servings: 4

Ingredients:
- Cabbage, shredded: 5 cups
- Smoked sausage, sliced: 14 oz
- Bell peppers, thinly sliced: 1 1/2 cups
- Onion, diced: 1 cup
- Garlic, chopped: 2 cloves
- Olive oil: 2 tablespoons
- Caraway seeds: 1 teaspoon
- Salt and pepper: to taste
- Fresh parsley: for garnishing

Instructions:
Shred the cabbage.

Slice the smoked sausage.

Thinly slice the bell peppers.

Dice the onion.

Chop the garlic.

Heat olive oil in a large skillet over medium heat.

Add the sliced sausage and cook until browned.

Stir in diced onion and chopped garlic.

Cook until the onion is translucent and the garlic is fragrant.

Add the shredded cabbage and sliced bell peppers to the skillet.

Sprinkle caraway seeds over the vegetables.

Season with salt and pepper to taste.

Continue to cook, stirring occasionally, until the cabbage is tender but still has a slight crunch.

Garnish with fresh parsley.

Serve hot and enjoy!

Nutritional Values (per serving): Calories 350 | Fat 25g | Carbohydrates 15g | Protein 18g

33. Greek Chicken Souvlaki Salad

Preparation Time: 20 minutes | Cooking Time: 15 minutes | Servings: 4

Ingredients:
- Boneless, skinless chicken breast, cut into bite-sized pieces: 1.1 lbs
- Cherry tomatoes, halved: 1 1/2 cups
- Cucumber, diced: 1 1/2 cups
- Red onion, thinly sliced: 1 cup
- Feta cheese, crumbled: 3/4 cup
- Kalamata olives, pitted and halved: 1/2 cup
- Olive oil: 2 tablespoons

- Red wine vinegar: 2 tablespoons
- Dried oregano: 1 teaspoon
- Garlic powder: 1 teaspoon
- Salt and pepper: to taste
For the Souvlaki Marinade:
- Greek yogurt: 3 tablespoons
- Olive oil: 2 tablespoons
- Lemon juice: 1 tablespoon
- Dried oregano: 2 teaspoons
- Garlic, chopped: 2 cloves
- Salt and pepper: to taste

Instructions:

In a bowl, mix the ingredients for the Souvlaki marinade. Add the chicken pieces, ensuring they are well coated. Marinate for at least 15 minutes.

While the chicken is marinating, prepare the salad ingredients. In a large bowl, mix the cherry tomatoes, cucumbers, red onions, feta cheese and Kalamata olives.

In a small bowl, whisk together olive oil, red wine vinegar, dried oregano, garlic powder, salt and pepper. Pour the dressing over the salad and gently toss.

Heat a grill or grill pan over medium-high heat. Skewer the marinated chicken pieces. Grill for about 12-15 minutes, turning occasionally, until the chicken is fully cooked and has a nice char.

Arrange the grilled chicken skewers on top of the prepared salad.

Nutritional Values (per serving): Calories 450 | Fat 25g | Carbohydrates 10g | Protein 45g

34.   Low-Carb Egg Drop Soup with Vegetables

Preparation Time: 10   minutes | Cooking Time: 15 minutes | Servings: 4

Ingredients:
- Chicken broth: 4 cups
- Mushrooms, sliced: 2 cups
- Spinach, chopped: 5 cups
- Green onions, finely chopped: 1 cup
- Eggs: 4 large
- Bamboo shoots, julienned: 1/2 cup
- Garlic, chopped: 2 cloves
- Ginger, grated: 1 teaspoon
- Soy sauce: 2 tablespoons
- Sesame oil: 1 tablespoon
- Salt and pepper: to taste
- Fresh cilantro: for garnishing

Instructions:
Simmer the chicken broth in a large pot over medium heat.

Add mushrooms, spinach, green onions, bamboo shoots, garlic and ginger to the pot. Cook the vegetables for about 5-7 minutes until soft.

Beat the eggs in a bowl and slowly pour them into the simmering soup while gently stirring with a fork. The eggs will form silky ribbons.

Season the soup with soy sauce, sesame oil, salt and pepper. Adjust seasoning to your taste.

Allow the soup to simmer for another 2-3 minutes to ensure the eggs are cooked.

Ladle the soup into bowls, garnish with fresh cilantro and serve hot.

Nutritional Values (per serving): Calories 120 | Fat 7g | Carbohydrates 5g | Protein 10g

35. Shrimp Avocado Ceviche in Lettuce Wraps

Preparation Time: 20   minutes | Cooking Time: 0 minutes | Servings: 2

Ingredients:
- Shrimp, peeled, deveined, and cooked: 7 oz
- Avocado, diced: 1 medium
- Tomato, diced: 1 cup
- Red onion, finely chopped: 1/3 cup
- Cilantro, chopped: 1/4 cup
- Jalapeño, deseeded and finely chopped: 1
- Juice of 2 limes
- Salt and pepper: to taste

- Large lettuce leaves (e.g., iceberg or butter lettuce): 6 leaves

Instructions:

In a bowl, mix the cooked shrimp, diced avocado, tomato, red onion, cilantro and Jalapeño.

Squeeze the lime juice over the mixture and season with salt and pepper. Gently toss until well combined.

Carefully wash and dry the lettuce leaves, making sure they are not too wet.

Spoon the shrimp avocado ceviche mixture onto each lettuce leaf and distribute evenly.

Serve immediately, allowing each person to wrap the ceviche in the lettuce leaves.

Nutritional Values (per serving): Calories 250 | Fat 12g | Carbohydrates 15g | Protein 20g

36. Roasted Brussels Sprouts and Bacon Salad

Preparation Time: 15 minutes | Cooking Time: 25 minutes | Servings: 4

Ingredients:

- Brussels sprouts, cleaned and halved: 4 cups
- Bacon, diced: 7 oz
- Almonds, chopped: 1/2 cup
- Parmesan cheese, grated: 1/2 cup
- Olive oil: 2 tablespoons
- Dijon mustard: 1 teaspoon
- Balsamic vinegar: 1 tablespoon
- Salt and pepper: to taste

Instructions:

Preheat the oven to 200°C (400°F).

In a large bowl, toss the Brussels sprouts with olive oil, salt and pepper until evenly coated.

Spread the Brussels sprouts in a single layer on a baking sheet. Roast in the preheated oven for 20-25 minutes, until golden brown and crispy at the edges.

While the Brussels sprouts are roasting, crisp the diced bacon in a skillet over medium heat. Remove excess fat by placing the cooked bacon on a paper towel.

In a small bowl, whisk together Dijon mustard and balsamic vinegar to prepare the dressing.

Once the Brussels sprouts are done, transfer them to a large bowl. Add the crispy bacon, sliced almonds and grated Parmesan cheese.

Pour the dressing over the salad and gently toss to ensure all ingredients are well mixed.

Serve the roasted Brussels sprouts and bacon salad warm, garnished with additional Parmesan if desired.

Nutritional Values (per serving): Calories 320 | Fat 24g | Carbohydrates 12g | Protein 15g

37. Chicken and Broccoli Alfredo Zoodles

Preparation Time: 15 minutes | Cooking Time: 15 minutes | Servings: 4

Ingredients:
- Zucchini, spiralized into zoodles: 4 cups
- Chicken breast, thinly sliced: 14 oz
- Broccoli florets: 3 cups
- Heavy cream: 3/4 cup
- Parmesan cheese, grated: 1 cup
- Unsalted butter: 1/4 cup
- Garlic, chopped: 2 cloves
- Salt and pepper: to taste
- Olive oil: for cooking

Instructions:
Spiralize the zucchini into zoodles.

Place the zoodles on a paper towel to absorb excess moisture.

Heat olive oil in a large skillet over medium heat.

Add the sliced chicken breast and cook until browned and fully cooked.

Add the broccoli florets and cook until tender yet crisp.

Season with salt and pepper to taste.

In a separate pot, melt the butter over medium heat.

Add the chopped garlic and sauté until fragrant.

Pour in the heavy cream and let it simmer slightly.

Stir in the Parmesan cheese until the sauce is smooth and creamy.

Add the prepared zoodles to the skillet with the chicken and broccoli.

Pour the Alfredo sauce over the zoodles and toss until well coated.

Cook for an additional 2 to 3 minutes until everything is heated through.

Nutritional Values (per serving): Calories 480 | Fat 34g | Carbohydrates 10g | Protein 35g

38. Tomato Basil Chicken from the Pot

Preparation Time: 10 minutes | Cooking Time: 20 minutes | Servings: 2

Ingredients:
- Boneless, skinless chicken breast, cut into bite-sized pieces: 1.1 lbs
- Cherry tomatoes, halved: 1 1/2 cups
- Fresh basil leaves, chopped: 1 1/2 cups
- Onion, finely diced: 1 cup

- Garlic, chopped: 3 cloves

- Chicken broth: 1 cup

- Zucchini, sliced: 2 cups

- Parmesan cheese, grated: 1 cup

- Olive oil: 2 tablespoons

- Salt and pepper: to taste

Instructions:

Heat olive oil in a large skillet over medium heat.

Add chopped onion and garlic and sauté until fragrant and translucent.

Season the chicken pieces with salt and pepper, add them to the skillet. Sauté until the chicken is browned on all sides.

Stir in the halved cherry tomatoes, sliced zucchini and chicken broth. Bring to a simmer and cook for 15-20 minutes, until the chicken is fully cooked.

Mix in the chopped fresh basil and stir well to distribute throughout.

Sprinkle grated Parmesan cheese over the top and let it melt.

Once the cheese has melted and the sauce has thickened, remove from heat.

Serve the tomato basil chicken in bowls, garnished with fresh basil as desired.

Nutritional Values (per serving): Calories 380 | Fat 18g | Carbohydrates 10g | Protein 42g

39. Spicy Tuna Avocado Wrap

Preparation Time: 15 minutes | Cooking Time: 0 minutes | Servings: 2

Ingredients:

- Canned tuna, drained: 7 oz

- Ripe avocado, pureed: 1 medium

- Mayonnaise: 2 tablespoons

- Sriracha sauce: 1 tablespoon

- Soy sauce: 1 teaspoon

- Large lettuce leaves: 4 leaves

- Cucumber, julienned: 1 1/4 cups

- Bell pepper, thinly sliced: 1 medium

- Nori sheets (seaweed): 4 sheets

- Salt and pepper: to taste

Instructions:

In a bowl, mix the drained tuna, mashed avocado, mayonnaise, Sriracha sauce and soy sauce. Mix well until all ingredients are evenly incorporated.

Lay out the Nori wrappers on a clean, flat surface.

Place a lettuce leaf on each Nori wrapper, leaving a margin at the edges.

Evenly distribute the tuna and avocado mixture on the lettuce leaves.

Sprinkle the julienned cucumber and sliced bell pepper over the tuna mixture.

Season with salt and pepper to taste.

Carefully roll the wraps from

one end to the other, enclosing the filling.

Moist the edge of the Nori wrapper with some water to seal the wrap.

Cut each wrap into bite-sized pieces with a sharp knife.

Serve immediately and enjoy the Spicy Tuna Avocado Wraps!

Nutritional Values (per serving): Calories 350 | Fat 20g | Carbohydrates 15g | Protein 25g

40. Creamy Avocado and Cucumber Gazpacho

Preparation Time: 15 minutes | Cooking Time: 0 minutes | Servings: 4

Ingredients:

- Ripe avocados, peeled and pitted: 2 medium (14 oz)
- Cucumber, peeled and diced: 2 cups (10.5 oz)
- Green bell pepper, diced: 1 cup (5.3 oz)
- Red onion, finely chopped: 1/3 cup (1.75 oz)
- Garlic, chopped: 2 cloves
- Greek yogurt: 1 cup (8.5 oz)
- Vegetable broth, chilled: 2 cups (16 oz)
- Olive oil: 1/4 cup (2 oz)
- Red wine vinegar: 3 tablespoons (1.5 oz)
- Salt and pepper: to taste
- Fresh cilantro or mint: for garnishing

Instructions:

Combine ripe avocados, diced cucumber, chopped bell pepper, finely chopped red onion, chopped garlic, Greek yogurt, chilled vegetable broth, olive oil and red wine vinegar in a blender.

Blend the ingredients until smooth and creamy. If the gazpacho is too thick, add more vegetable broth until you reach the desired consistency.

Season the gazpacho with salt and pepper to taste. Blend again to ensure the spices are evenly distributed.

Once the gazpacho has reached the desired consistency and flavor, transfer it to a large bowl and refrigerate for at least one hour to allow the flavors to meld.

Stir the gazpacho well before serving. Divide into four servings.

Garnish each serving with fresh cilantro or mint.

Nutritional Values (per serving): Calories 250 | Fat 18g | Carbohydrates 18g | Protein 5g

Chapter 6: Dinner

41. Baked Salmon with Dill and Asparagus Spears

Preparation Time: 20 minutes | Cooking Time: 20 minutes | Servings: 2

Ingredients:

- Salmon fillets: 14 oz

- Asparagus spears, trimmed: 2 cups

- Olive oil: 2 tablespoons

- Garlic cloves, chopped: 2 cloves

- Fresh dill, chopped: 1 tablespoon

- Lemon, sliced: 1

- Salt and pepper: to taste

Instructions:

Preheat the oven to 200°C (400°F).

Place the salmon fillets on a parchment-lined baking sheet. Arrange the asparagus spears around the salmon.

Drizzle olive oil over the salmon and asparagus. Sprinkle chopped garlic and chopped dill evenly over the salmon fillets.

Season with salt and pepper. Place lemon slices on top of the salmon.

Bake in the preheated oven for 20 minutes or until the salmon is cooked through and flakes easily with a fork.

Remove from the oven and let rest for a few minutes.

Serve the baked salmon alongside asparagus spears. Squeeze fresh lemon juice over the dish to enhance the flavors.

Nutritional Values (per serving): Calories 450 | Fat 28g | Carbohydrates 5g | Protein 40g

42. Grilled Lemon-Herb Chicken with Zucchini Noodles

Preparation Time: 15 minutes | Cooking Time: 20 minutes | Servings: 4

Ingredients:

- Boneless, skinless chicken breast: 1.3 lbs
- Zucchinis, spiralized into noodles: 4 medium (about 4 cups)
- Juice and zest of 2 lemons
- Garlic cloves, chopped: 3 cloves
- Fresh parsley, chopped: 2 tablespoons
- Fresh thyme, chopped: 2 tablespoons
- Olive oil: 2 tablespoons
- Salt and pepper: to taste

Instructions:

Warm up the grill to medium-high heat.

Marinate the chicken: in a bowl, combine olive oil, lemon juice, lemon zest, chopped garlic, chopped parsley, chopped thyme, salt and pepper. Mix well.

Place the chicken breasts in a resealable plastic bag or a flat dish and pour half of the marinade over them, saving the other half for later. Ensure the chicken is evenly coated. Marinate in the refrigerator for at least 30 minutes.

Grill the Chicken: Remove the chicken from the marinade and grill for about 8-10 minutes on each side or until the internal temperature reaches 165°F (74°C) and the chicken has nice grill marks.

While the chicken is grilling, heat a large pan over medium heat. Add the spiralized zucchini noodles and sauté for 3 to 4 minutes, until just tender but still slightly crunchy. Set aside.

Once the chicken is cooked, let it rest for a few minutes before slicing it into thin strips. Toss the zucchini noodles with the reserved marinade.

Serve the grilled lemon-herb chicken on a bed of zucchini noodles.

Nutritional Values (per serving): **Calories 320 | Fat 12g | Carbohydrates 12g | Protein 40g**

43. Cauliflower and Broccoli Alfredo Casserole

Preparation Time: 20 minutes | Cooking Time: 30 minutes | Servings: 4

Ingredients:

- Cauliflower, cut into florets: 4 cups
- Broccoli, cut into florets: 4 cups
- Cream cheese: 7 oz
- Heavy cream: 1 cup
- Grated Parmesan cheese: 1 cup
- Garlic cloves, chopped: 2 cloves
- Onion powder: 1 teaspoon
- Grated nutmeg: 1/2 teaspoon
- Salt and pepper: to taste
- Mozzarella cheese, shredded: 1 1/2 cups
- Fresh parsley, chopped: for garnishing

Instructions:

Preheat the oven to 200°C (180°C fan).

In a large pot of boiling salted water, cook the cauliflower and broccoli for about 5-7 minutes until they are soft. Drain and set aside.

In a saucepan over medium heat, combine cream cheese, heavy cream, Parmesan cheese, chopped garlic, onion powder, nutmeg, salt and pepper. Stir continuously until the mixture is smooth and well combined.

Place the cooked cauliflower and broccoli in a baking dish and pour the Alfredo sauce over the vegetables. Gently stir to ensure the vegetables are evenly coated.

Sprinkle the shredded mozzarella cheese on top.

Bake in the preheated oven for 20-25 minutes until the cheese is melted and the edges are golden brown.

Remove from the oven and let it cool for a few minutes before serving.

Garnish with chopped fresh parsley and serve hot.

Nutritional Values (per serving): Calories 450 | Fat 35g | Carbohydrates 15g | Protein 18g

44. Spicy Shrimp Stir-Fry with Shirataki Noodles

Preparation Time: 15 minutes | Cooking Time: 15 minutes | Servings: 2

Ingredients:
- Shrimp, peeled and deveined: 10.5 oz
- Shirataki noodles: 7 oz
- Broccoli florets: 1 1/2 cups
- Bell peppers, thinly sliced: 1 cup
- Snap peas, trimmed: 1/2 cup
- Vegetable oil: 2 tablespoons
- Garlic cloves, chopped: 3 cloves
- Ginger, grated: 1 tablespoon
- Soy sauce: 2 tablespoons
- Chili garlic sauce: 1 tablespoon
- Sesame oil: 1 teaspoon
- Rice vinegar: 1 teaspoon
- Erythritol (or your choice of low-carb sweetener): 1 teaspoon
- Salt and pepper: to taste
- Fresh cilantro: for garnishing

Instructions:

Prepare Shirataki noodles: rinse the shirataki noodles under cold water and blanch them for 2-3 minutes in hot water. Drain and set aside.

Cook shrimp: in a large pan or wok, heat 1 tablespoon of vegetable oil over medium-high heat. Add the shrimp and fry until they turn pink, about 2-3 minutes per side. Remove the shrimp from the pan and set aside.

Stir-fry vegetables: add the remaining tablespoon of vegetable oil to the same pan. Stir in chopped garlic and grated ginger until fragrant. Add broccoli, bell peppers and snap peas. Stir-fry for 3-4 minutes until the vegetables are tender yet crisp.

Combine ingredients: return the cooked shirataki noodles and cooked shrimp to the pan. Stir in soy sauce, chili garlic sauce, sesame oil, rice vinegar and erythritol. Mix everything together until well combined and heated through.

Adjust seasoning: season with salt and pepper to taste. Adjust the level of spiciness and sweetness as desired.

Serve: divide the spicy shrimp with shirataki noodles onto two plates. Garnish with fresh cilantro.

Nutritional Values (per serving): Calories 320 | Fat 15g | Carbohydrates 10g | Protein 30g

45. Pesto Turkey Meatballs with Roasted Brussels Sprouts

Preparation Time: 15 minutes | Cooking Time: 25 minutes | Servings: 4

Ingredients:
- Ground turkey: 1.1 lbs
- Almond flour: 1 cup
- Grated Parmesan cheese: 1/4 cup
- Fresh basil, finely chopped: 1/4 cup
- Garlic cloves, chopped: 2 cloves
- Egg: 1 large
- Salt and pepper: to taste
- Brussels sprouts, halved: 4 cups
- Olive oil: 2 tablespoons
- Pesto sauce (store-bought or homemade): 1/4 cup

Instructions:
Preheat the oven to 200°C (400°F).

In a large mixing bowl, combine ground turkey, almond flour, Parmesan, chopped basil, chopped garlic, egg, salt and pepper. Mix well until all ingredients are evenly incorporated.

Form the mixture into meatballs about 1.5 cm in diameter and place them on a parchment paper-lined baking sheet.

Toss the halved Brussels sprouts with olive oil, salt and pepper. Arrange around the meatballs on the baking sheet.

Bake in the preheated oven for 20-25 minutes, until the meatballs are cooked through and golden and the Brussels sprouts are roasted and slightly crispy.

While the meatballs and Brussels sprouts are baking, warm the pesto sauce in a small pot over low heat.

Once the meatballs and Brussels sprouts are done, drizzle the pesto sauce over the meatballs.

Serve the pesto turkey meatballs on a bed of roasted Brussels sprouts.

Nutritional Values (per serving): Calories 450 | Fat 28g | Carbohydrates 10g | Protein 40g

46. Eggplant Lasagna with Ground Turkey and Spinach

Preparation Time: 20 minutes | Cooking Time: 40 minutes | Servings: 4

Ingredients:
- Eggplants, sliced thinly: 1.3 lbs
- Ground turkey: 14 oz
- Fresh spinach, chopped: 2 cups
- Ricotta cheese: 14 oz
- Mozzarella cheese, shredded: 2 cups
- Parmesan cheese, grated: 1 cup
- Crushed tomatoes (1 can): 14 oz
- Garlic cloves, chopped: 2 cloves
- Dried oregano: 1 teaspoon
- Dried basil: 1 teaspoon
- Salt and pepper: to taste
- Olive oil: for cooking

Instructions:
Preheat the oven to 180°C (350°F).

In a large skillet, heat the olive oil over medium heat. Add chopped garlic and sauté until fragrant.

Add the ground turkey to the skillet and cook until browned. Season with salt, pepper, dried oregano and dried basil. Stir in the crushed tomatoes and simmer for 10 minutes.

In a separate pan, lightly sauté the sliced eggplants until soft. Set aside.

In a bowl, mix together ricotta, half of the mozzarella and half of the Parmesan. Mix well.

Layer half of the cooked eggplant slices in a baking dish. Spread half of the turkey-tomato mixture over the eggplants.

Sprinkle half of the chopped spinach over the turkey mixture.

Spread half of the cheese mixture over the spinach layer and distribute evenly.

Repeat the layers with the remaining ingredients, finishing with a cheese layer.

Cover the baking dish with foil and bake in the preheated oven for 30 minutes. Then remove the foil and bake for an additional 10 minutes or until the cheese is golden and bubbly.

Nutritional Values (per serving): Calories 480 | Fat 28g | Carbohydrates 15g | Protein 40g

47. Lemon Garlic Butter Cod with Cauliflower Rice

Preparation Time: 15 minutes | Cooking Time: 20 minutes | Servings: 4

Ingredients:
- Cod fillets: 1.3 lbs
- Cauliflower, riced: 6 cups
- Unsalted butter: 7 tablespoons
- Garlic cloves, chopped: 4 cloves
- Lemon, juiced and zested: 1
- Fresh parsley, chopped: 2 tablespoons
- Salt and pepper: to taste

Instructions:
Prepare the cod: pat the cod fillets dry with a paper towel and season with salt and pepper.

In a large skillet, melt 50g of butter over medium heat.

Add the cod fillets and cook for 4-5 minutes per side or until the fish flakes easily with a fork.

After cooking, squeeze half of the lemon over the cod and set aside.

Prepare the cauliflower rice: in the same skillet, add the remaining butter and the chopped garlic.

Sauté the garlic until fragrant, then add the riced cauliflower.

Cook for 5-7 minutes, until the cauliflower is tender but not mushy.

Stir in the lemon zest and juice from the remaining lemon half.

Season with salt and pepper to taste.

Serve:

Divide the cauliflower rice among four plates.

Place a cod fillet on each plate.

Sprinkle fresh parsley over the top for garnish.

Nutritional Values (per serving): Calories 380 | Fat 18g | Carbohydrates 10g | Protein 45g

48. Stuffed Portobello Mushrooms with Spinach and Feta

Preparation Time: 15 minutes | Cooking Time: 25 minutes | Servings: 2

Ingredients:

- Portobello mushrooms (approx. 400g): 4 large
- Fresh spinach, chopped: 2 cups
- Feta cheese, crumbled: 1/2 cup
- Small onion, finely chopped: 1/2 cup
- Garlic cloves, chopped: 2 cloves
- Pine nuts, toasted: 1/4 cup
- Olive oil: 2 tablespoons
- Dried oregano: 1 teaspoon
- Salt and pepper: to taste
- Fresh parsley: for garnishing

Instructions:

Preheat the oven to 200°C (400°F).

Clean the Portobello mushrooms and remove their stems. Place them on a baking sheet.

Heat 1 tablespoon of olive oil in a skillet over medium heat. Add the chopped onion and garlic and sauté until soft.

Add the chopped spinach to the skillet and cook until wilted. Season with salt, pepper and dried oregano.

In a bowl, mix the crumbled feta cheese and toasted pine nuts. Add the sautéed spinach mixture and mix well.

Brush the mushroom caps with the remaining olive oil and place them on the baking sheet.

Fill each mushroom cap with the spinach-feta mixture, pressing down lightly.

Bake in the preheated oven for about 20-25 minutes until the mushrooms are tender.

Garnish with fresh parsley before serving.

Nutritional Values (per serving): Calories 220 | Fat 15g | Carbohydrates 10g | Protein 12g

49. Garlic Parmesan Chicken with Pan-Roasted Vegetables

Preparation Time: 15 minutes | Cooking Time: 25 minutes | Servings: 4

Ingredients:

- Boneless, skinless chicken breast, sliced into strips: 1.1 lbs
- Broccoli florets: 4 cups
- Cherry tomatoes, halved: 2 cups
- Green beans, trimmed: 2 cups
- Grated Parmesan cheese: 1/2 cup
- Garlic cloves, chopped: 4 cloves

- Olive oil: 3 tablespoons

- Dried oregano: 1 teaspoon

- Dried thyme: 1 teaspoon

- Salt and black pepper: to taste

- Fresh parsley, chopped: for garnishing

Instructions:

Preheat the oven to 220°C (425°F).

In a large mixing bowl, combine the chicken strips, broccoli florets, cherry tomatoes and green beans.

In a small bowl, whisk together the chopped garlic, olive oil, dried oregano, dried thyme, salt and black pepper.

Drizzle the garlic-herb mixture over the chicken and vegetables. Toss everything together until well coated.

Spread the chicken and vegetables evenly on a large baking sheet.

Sprinkle the grated Parmesan cheese over the chicken and vegetables.

Bake in the preheated oven for 25 minutes, until the chicken is cooked through and the vegetables are tender.

Remove from the oven and garnish with fresh chopped parsley before serving.

Nutritional Values (per serving): Calories 380 | Fat 18g | Carbohydrates 12g | Protein 42g

50. Beef Enchiladas in Cabbage Wrap

Preparation Time: 20 minutes | Cooking Time: 40 minutes | Servings: 4

Ingredients:

- Ground beef: 1.8 lbs

- White cabbage: 1 medium-sized (approx. 2 lbs), shredded

- Onion, finely diced: 1 cup

- Garlic cloves, chopped: 2 cloves

- Bell pepper, diced: 1 cup

- Diced tomatoes: 1 can

- Chili powder: 2 teaspoons

- Cumin: 1 teaspoon

- Paprika: 1 teaspoon

- Salt and pepper: to taste

- Shredded cheese (Cheddar or Mexican blend): 2 cups

Instructions:

Bring a large pot of water to a boil.

Carefully detach the cabbage leaves and blanch in boiling water for 2-3 minutes until they become pliable.

Remove the leaves and set aside to cool.

In a large skillet over medium heat, brown the ground beef.

Add chopped onions, chopped garlic and diced bell pepper. Cook until the vegetables are soft.

Stir in diced tomatoes, chili powder, cumin, paprika, salt and pepper. Simmer for 10-15 minutes until flavors meld.

Preheat the oven to 180°C (350°F).

Take a cabbage leaf and spoon a generous amount of the beef mixture into the center.

Roll it up and tuck in the sides, similar to a burrito.

Place the cabbage-wrapped enchiladas seam side down in a baking dish.

Sprinkle the grated cheese over the enchiladas.

Bake in the preheated oven for 20-25 minutes until the cheese is melted and bubbly.

Remove from the oven and let cool for a few minutes before serving.

Nutritional Values (per serving): Calories 480 | Fat 28g | Carbohydrates 12g | Protein 44g

51. Teriyaki Glazed Tofu Skewers with Grilled Vegetables

Preparation Time: 15 minutes | Cooking Time: 15 minutes | Servings: 2

Ingredients:
- Extra-firm tofu, pressed and cubed: 14 oz
- Cherry tomatoes: 1 1/2 cups
- Bell peppers, diced: 1 1/2 cups
- Zucchini, sliced: 2 cups
- Red onion, cut into wedges: 1 medium

For the Teriyaki Glaze:
- Soy sauce: 4 tablespoons
- Mirin: 2 tablespoons
- Sake: 2 tablespoons
- Rice vinegar: 1 tablespoon
- Erythritol (or sweetener of choice): 2 tablespoons
- Grated ginger: 1 teaspoon
- Garlic, chopped: 2 cloves
- Sesame oil: 1 tablespoon

Instructions:
Prepare the Teriyaki glaze: in a small pot, mix soy sauce, Mirin, Sake, rice vinegar, erythritol, grated ginger, chopped garlic and sesame oil.

Simmer over low heat for 5-7 minutes until the glaze thickens. Set aside.

Prepare tofu and vegetables: thread tofu cubes, cherry tomatoes, bell peppers, zucchini and red onions onto skewers.

Grill the skewers: preheat the grill or grill pan to medium-high heat.

Place skewers on the grill and brush with the prepared Teriyaki glaze.

Grill for 8-10 minutes, turning occasionally, until tofu is golden brown and vegetables are charred.

Remove skewers from the grill and brush with additional Teriyaki glaze.

Serve immediately, optionally garnished with sesame seeds and chopped green onions.

Nutritional Values (per serving): Calories 280 | Fat 15g | Carbohydrates 20g | Protein 18g

52. Keto-Friendly Greek Salad with Grilled Chicken

Preparation Time: 15 minutes | Cooking Time: 15 minutes | Servings: 2

Ingredients:
- Boneless, skinless chicken breasts: 14 oz
- Cherry tomatoes, halved: 1 1/2 cups
- Cucumber, diced: 1 cup
- Feta cheese, crumbled: 1 cup
- Black olives, pitted and sliced: 3/4 cup
- Red onions, thinly sliced: 1/2 cup
- Green bell pepper, diced: 1/3 cup
- Extra virgin olive oil: 2 tablespoons
- Red wine vinegar: 1 tablespoon
- Fresh oregano, chopped: 1 tablespoon
- Salt and pepper: to taste

Instructions:
Preheat the grill to medium-high heat.
Season chicken breasts with salt and pepper.
Grill for about 6-8 minutes per side or until cooked through.
Let the chicken rest for 5 minutes before slicing it into strips.
In a large bowl, mix cherry tomatoes, cucumbers, feta cheese, olives, red onions and green bell pepper.
In a small bowl, whisk together extra virgin olive oil, red wine vinegar, chopped oregano, salt and pepper.
Arrange the sliced grilled chicken over the salad.
Pour the dressing over the salad and gently toss to combine.
Distribute the salad onto plates and serve immediately.

Nutritional Values (per serving): Calories 380 | Fat 22g | Carbohydrates 10g | Protein 36g

53. Spaghetti Squash Carbonara with Bacon and Peas

Preparation Time: 15 minutes | Cooking Time: 30 minutes | Servings: 4

Ingredients:
- Spaghetti squash: 1 medium (approx. 2.2 lbs)

- Bacon, diced: 7 oz
- Frozen peas: 1 cup
- Eggs: 4 large
- Parmesan cheese, grated: 1 cup
- Garlic cloves, chopped: 2 cloves
- Salt and black pepper: to taste
- Fresh parsley, chopped: for garnish

Instructions:

Preheat the oven: set the oven to 200°C (400°F).

Prepare the spaghetti squash: halve the spaghetti squash lengthwise and remove the seeds. Place the halves cut-side down on a baking sheet. Bake in the preheated oven for 25-30 minutes or until the squash is soft.

While the squash is baking, crisp the diced bacon in a large pan over medium heat. Remove the bacon from the pan and drain it on a paper towel-lined plate.

In the same pan, sauté the chopped garlic until fragrant. Add the frozen peas and cook until heated through. Remove the pan from the heat.

In a bowl, whisk together the eggs and grated Parmesan cheese. Set aside.

Once the spaghetti squash is cooked, use a fork to shred the flesh into strands. Add the spaghetti strands to the pan with the peas and garlic.

Combine with egg mixture: pour the egg-cheese mixture over the spaghetti, tossing quickly to coat the strands. The residual heat will cook the eggs, creating a creamy sauce.

Return the crispy bacon to the pan, reserving some for garnish. Season with salt and black pepper.

Garnish with chopped fresh parsley and the reserved bacon bits.

Nutritional Values (per serving): **Calories 320 | Fat 20g | Carbohydrates 15g | Protein 18g**

54. Lemon Butter Shrimp and Broccoli Patties

Preparation Time: 15 minutes | Cooking Time: 15 minutes | Servings: 4

Ingredients:
- Shrimp, peeled and deveined: 1 pound
- Broccoli, cut into florets: 4 cups
- Unsalted butter: 1/4 cup
- Olive oil: 2 tablespoons
- Garlic cloves, chopped: 4 cloves
- Red pepper flakes (optional): 1 teaspoon
- Lemon zest: 1 teaspoon
- Lemon juice: 3 tablespoons
- Salt and pepper: to taste

- Fresh parsley, chopped: for garnish

Instructions:

Ensure the shrimp are peeled and deveined. Cut broccoli into florets. Chop the garlic. Zest the lemon and squeeze out the juice.

In a large pan, heat olive oil and 30g of butter over medium heat.

Add chopped garlic and red pepper flakes (if using). Sauté until fragrant.

Add the shrimp to the pan and cook for 2-3 minutes on each side, until they turn pink. Remove the shrimp from the pan and set aside.

In the same pan, add the remaining butter and the broccoli florets. Sauté until the broccoli is tender yet still crisp.

Return the cooked shrimp to the pan.

Add lemon zest and lemon juice, tossing everything together evenly.

Season with salt and pepper to taste.

Garnish with chopped fresh parsley.

Nutritional Values (per serving): **Calories 320 | Fat 22g | Carbohydrates 8g | Protein 25g**

55. Turkey Zucchini Skillet with Creamy Tomato Sauce

Preparation Time: 15 minutes | Cooking Time: 20 minutes | Servings: 4

Ingredients:
- Ground turkey: 1 pound
- Zucchini, sliced into rounds: 3 cups
- Cherry tomatoes, halved: 2 cups
- Small onion, finely diced: 1/2 cup
- Garlic cloves, chopped: 2 cloves
- Tomato sauce: 1 cup
- Cream: 1/2 cup
- Grated Parmesan cheese: 1/2 cup
- Olive oil: 2 tablespoons
- Dried oregano: 1 teaspoon
- Dried basil: 1 teaspoon
- Salt and pepper: to taste

Instructions:

Heat olive oil in a large skillet over medium heat.

Add chopped onions and garlic, sautéing until fragrant.

Add ground turkey to the skillet, breaking it apart with a spoon and cook until browned.

Stir in sliced zucchini and halved cherry tomatoes. Cook for another 5 minutes until the vegetables are slightly softened.

Mix in tomato sauce, dried oregano and dried basil. Season with salt and pepper to taste. Stir well to combine everything.

Reduce heat to low, add the cream and simmer for 5-7 minutes until the sauce thickens.

Sprinkle grated Parmesan cheese over the skillet and let it melt into the sauce.

Once the cheese is melted and the sauce has thickened, remove the skillet from the heat.

Serve hot, dividing the contents of the skillet among four plates.

Nutritional Values (per serving): Calories 450 | Fat 25g | Carbohydrates 12g | Protein 35g

56. Grilled Swordfish Steaks with Cilantro-Lime Cauliflower Rice

Preparation Time: 15 minutes | Cooking Time: 20 minutes | Servings: 4

Ingredients:
- Swordfish steaks: 4 (1.3 pounds)
- Cauliflower, diced: 4 cups
- Olive oil: 1/4 cup
- Garlic cloves, chopped: 4 cloves
- Fresh cilantro, chopped: 1/4 cup
- Juice of 2 limes: 1/2 cup
- Salt and pepper: to taste
- Lemon wedges: for serving

Instructions:
Heat your grill to medium-high heat.

Pat the swordfish steaks dry with paper towels.

Season both sides with salt and pepper.

Place the swordfish steaks on the preheated grill.

Grill each side for about 4-5 minutes or until the fish is opaque and easily flakes with a fork.

In a large skillet, heat the olive oil over medium heat.

Add the chopped garlic and sauté until fragrant.

Stir in the diced cauliflower and cook for 5-7 minutes, stirring occasionally.

Mix in the chopped cilantro and lime juice.

Cook for another 2-3 minutes, until the cauliflower is tender.

Season with salt and pepper to taste.

Place a generous portion of cilantro-lime cauliflower rice on each plate.

Top with the grilled swordfish steaks.

Garnish with additional cilantro and serve with lemon wedges on the side.

Nutritional Values (per serving): Calories 400 | Fat 20g | Carbohydrates 10g | Protein 40g

57. Cheesy Portobello Mushroom Caps with Ground Turkey

Preparation Time: 15 minutes | Cooking Time: 25 minutes | Servings: 2

Ingredients:

- Large Portobello mushroom caps: 4 (approx. 14 oz)
- Lean ground turkey: 9 oz
- Olive oil: 1 tablespoon
- Small onion, finely chopped: 1/2 cup
- Garlic cloves, chopped: 2 cloves
- Dried oregano: 1/2 teaspoon
- Dried thyme: 1/2 teaspoon
- Salt and pepper: to taste
- Grated mozzarella cheese: 1/2 cup
- Grated Parmesan cheese: 2 tablespoons
- Fresh parsley: for garnishing (optional)

Instructions:

Preheat the oven to 200°C (400°F).

Clean the Portobello mushroom caps and remove the stems. Place them on a baking sheet lined with parchment paper.

In a skillet over medium heat, heat the olive oil. Sauté the chopped onions until translucent, then add the chopped garlic and cook for another 1-2 minutes.

Add the ground turkey to the skillet and cook until browned. Season with dried oregano, dried thyme, salt and pepper. Stir well to combine.

Evenly fill the mushroom caps with the turkey mixture, pressing down lightly.

Sprinkle each stuffed mushroom cap with grated mozzarella and Parmesan cheese.

Bake in the preheated oven for 20-25 minutes, until the cheese is melted and the mushrooms are tender.

Garnish with fresh parsley if desired.

Nutritional Values (per serving): Calories 320 | Fat 18g | Carbohydrates 9g | Protein 30g

58. Buffalo Chicken Lettuce Wraps with Avocado

Preparation Time: 15 minutes | Cooking Time: 15 minutes | Servings: 2-4

Ingredients:

- Cooked and shredded chicken breast: 14 oz
- Buffalo sauce: 2/3 cup
- Butter: 2 tablespoons
- Garlic powder: 1 teaspoon
- Onion powder: 1 teaspoon
- Salt and pepper: to taste

- Large lettuce leaves (e.g., iceberg or romaine): 8 leaves
- Ripe avocado, sliced: 1 medium
- Blue cheese, crumbled: 1/4 cup
- Celery, finely chopped: 1/4 cup
- Low-carb ranch dressing: 2 tablespoons

Instructions:

Cook the chicken breast until fully cooked.

Shred the chicken into bite-sized pieces.

In a pot, melt the butter and add buffalo sauce, garlic powder, onion powder, salt and pepper.

Stir well until everything is well combined.

Add the shredded chicken to the sauce and mix to evenly coat.

Simmer for 5 minutes until the chicken has absorbed the flavors.

Lay out the large lettuce leaves on a flat surface.

Spoon the buffalo chicken mixture onto each lettuce leaf.

Top with slices of avocado, crumbled blue cheese and chopped celery.

Drizzle with Ranch Dressing:

Drizzle the low-carb ranch dressing over the completed wraps.

Carefully fold the lettuce leaves to form wraps.

Serve immediately and secure the wraps with toothpicks if necessary.

Nutritional Values (per serving): Calories 320 | Fat 18g | Carbohydrates 8g | Protein 30g

59. Sesame Ginger Tofu Stir-Fry with Low-Carb Noodles

Preparation Time: 15 minutes | Cooking Time: 15 minutes | Servings: 4

Ingredients:

- Tofu, pressed and cubed: 14 oz
- Low-carb noodles: 7 oz
- Broccoli florets: 1 1/2 cups
- Snap peas, trimmed: 1 cup
- Red bell pepper, thinly sliced: 1 cup
- Sesame oil: 2 tablespoons
- Low-sodium soy sauce: 3 tablespoons
- Rice vinegar: 2 tablespoons
- Fresh ginger, grated: 1 tablespoon
- Garlic, chopped: 2 cloves
- Sesame seeds: 1 tablespoon
- Green onions, sliced: 2
- Salt and pepper: to taste

Instructions:

Prepare the tofu: press the tofu to remove excess water, then cut it into bite-sized cubes.

Cook the low-carb noodles: cook the low-carb noodles according to the package instructions. Drain and set aside.

Stir-fry the vegetables: heat 1 tablespoon of sesame oil in a large wok or pan over medium-high heat.

Add broccoli, snap peas and red bell pepper. Stir-fry for 3-4 minutes until the vegetables are tender but still crisp. Remove from the pan and set aside.

Cook the tofu: add another tablespoon of sesame oil to the same pan.

Add the tofu cubes and fry until golden brown on all sides, about 5-6 minutes.

Prepare the sauce: in a small bowl, mix soy sauce, rice vinegar, grated ginger and chopped garlic.

Combine ingredients: add the cooked noodles, stir-fried vegetables and tofu back to the pan.

Pour the sauce over the mixture and toss until everything is well-coated and heated through.

Finish and serve: sprinkle sesame seeds and sliced green onions on top.

Season with salt and pepper if needed.

Serve immediately.

Nutritional Values (per serving): Calories 380 | Fat 18g | Carbohydrates 28g | Protein 24g

60. Baked Tilapia with Parmesan Crust and Roasted Asparagus

Preparation Time: 15 minutes | Cooking Time: 20 minutes | Servings: 2-4

Ingredients:
- Tilapia fillets: 14 oz
- Asparagus spears, trimmed: 2 cups
- Grated Parmesan cheese: 1/2 cup
- Almond flour: 1/4 cup
- Olive oil: 2 tablespoons
- Fresh parsley, chopped: 2 tablespoons
- Garlic powder: 1 teaspoon
- Lemon zest: 1 teaspoon
- Salt and pepper: to taste

Instructions:
Preheat the oven to 200°C (400°F).

In a bowl, mix grated Parmesan cheese, almond flour, chopped parsley, garlic powder, lemon zest, salt and pepper.

Pat the tilapia fillets dry and coat each fillet evenly with the Parmesan mixture, pressing it onto the fillets.

Place the coated tilapia fillets on a baking sheet lined with parchment paper. Drizzle olive oil over the fillets.

Arrange the trimmed asparagus spears on the same baking sheet, drizzle with olive oil and season with salt and pepper.

Bake in the preheated oven for 15-20 minutes, until the tilapia is cooked through and the coating is golden brown. The asparagus should be tender yet slightly crisp. While baking, prepare a simple side salad or additional vegetables, if desired.

Serve the baked tilapia with Parmesan crust alongside the roasted asparagus.

Nutritional Values (per serving): Calories 350 | Fat 20g | Carbohydrates 5g | Protein 35g

Chapter 7: Snacks

61. Crispy Kale Chips

Preparation Time: 10 minutes | Cooking Time: 20 minutes | Servings: 2

Ingredients:

- Fresh kale, washed and thoroughly dried: 10 cups
- Olive oil: 1 tablespoon
- Nutritional yeast: 1 tablespoon
- Garlic powder: 1 teaspoon
- Onion powder: 1 teaspoon
- Smoked paprika: 1/2 teaspoon
- Salt and pepper: to taste

Instructions:

Preheat the oven to 150°C (300°F).

Remove the tough stems from the kale leaves and tear the leaves into bite-sized pieces.

In a large bowl, toss the kale with the olive oil to ensure each piece is evenly coated.

Sprinkle nutritional yeast, garlic powder, onion powder, smoked paprika, salt and pepper over the kale. Toss well to distribute the spices evenly.

Spread the kale in a single layer on a baking sheet lined with parchment paper.

Bake in the preheated oven for 15-20 minutes, until the edges are crispy but not burnt. Keep a close eye on them as cooking times may vary.

Remove from the oven and let the kale chips cool on the baking sheet for a few minutes to become even crispier.

Transfer the crispy kale chips to a serving bowl and enjoy them as a delicious snack or side dish.

Nutritional Values (per serving): Calories 75 | Fat 4g | Carbohydrates 9g | Protein 4g

62. Spicy Avocado and Cucumber Bites

Preparation Time: 15 minutes | Cooking Time: 0 minutes | Servings: 4

Ingredients:

- Ripe avocados: 2 (approx. 14 oz)
- Cucumber: 1 1/2 cups
- Fresh lime juice: 1 tablespoon
- Fresh cilantro, chopped: 2 tablespoons
- Garlic clove, chopped: 1 clove
- Salt and pepper: to taste
- Cherry tomatoes, diced: 1/2 cup
- Feta cheese, crumbled: 1/4 cup

Instructions:

Peel and pit the avocados, then cut them into small, bite-sized pieces.

Slice the cucumber thinly or peel and dice it into small cubes.

In a medium-sized bowl, mix the diced avocados and cucumbers.

Add fresh lime juice, chopped cilantro, chopped garlic, salt and pepper to the bowl. Gently toss the ingredients until well combined.

Carefully fold in the diced cherry tomatoes, ensuring they are evenly distributed throughout the mixture.

Sprinkle the crumbled feta cheese on top, providing a tangy contrast to the creamy avocados.

Serve immediately as a refreshing and low-carb appetizer or snack.

Nutritional Values (per serving): Calories 180 | Fat 15g | Carbohydrates 10g | Protein 4g

63. Spicy Roasted Almonds with Sea Salt

Preparation Time: 10 minutes | Cooking Time: 15 minutes | Servings: 4

Ingredients:

- Raw almonds: 3 cups
- Olive oil: 2 tablespoons
- Smoked paprika: 1 teaspoon
- Cayenne pepper: 1/2 teaspoon
- Garlic powder: 1 teaspoon
- Onion powder: 1 teaspoon
- Sea salt (or to taste): 1 teaspoon

Instructions:

Preheat the oven to 160°C (320°F).

In a large bowl, mix the raw almonds with olive oil, smoked paprika, cayenne pepper, garlic powder and onion powder. Toss until the almonds are evenly coated with the spice mixture.

Spread the seasoned almonds in a single layer on a baking sheet lined with parchment paper.

Roast the almonds in the preheated oven for 15 minutes, stirring halfway through, until they are golden brown and fragrant.

Remove the almonds from the oven and immediately sprinkle with sea salt. Toss the almonds again to ensure they are evenly coated.

Let the spicy roasted almonds cool completely before transferring them to an airtight container.

Nutritional Values (per serving): Calories 230 | Fat 20g | Carbohydrates 7g | Protein 8g

64. Cheesy Cauliflower Bites

Preparation Time: 15 minutes | Cooking Time: 25 minutes | Servings: 4

Ingredients:
- Cauliflower, cut into florets: 4 cups
- Shredded cheddar cheese: 1 1/2 cups
- Almond flour: 1/2 cup
- Eggs: 2 large
- Grated Parmesan cheese: 1/2 cup
- Garlic powder: 1 teaspoon
- Onion powder: 1 teaspoon
- Dried oregano: 1/2 teaspoon
- Salt and pepper: to taste
- Cooking spray: as needed

Instructions:

Preheat the oven to 200°C (180°C fan-forced) and line a baking sheet with parchment paper.

Steam the cauliflower florets in a large pot until fork-tender, about 8-10 minutes.

Once the cauliflower is cooked, transfer it to a clean kitchen towel and allow it to cool slightly. Pat the cauliflower dry to remove excess moisture.

In a large bowl, combine cauliflower, shredded cheddar cheese, almond flour, Parmesan, garlic powder, onion powder, dried oregano, salt and pepper. Mix until all ingredients are well combined.

Beat the eggs in a separate bowl. Add the beaten eggs to the cauliflower mixture and stir until a sticky dough forms.

Use your hands to form the dough into bite-sized balls and place them on the prepared baking sheet, ensuring some space between each bite.

Lightly spray the top of the cauliflower bites with cooking spray to help them brown in the oven.

Bake in the preheated oven for 15-18 minutes, until the bites are firm and golden.

Remove from the oven and allow to cool for a few minutes before serving.

Nutritional Values (per serving): Calories 220 | Fat 15g | Carbohydrates 8g | Protein 12g

65. Mediterranean Vegetable Skewers with Feta Dip

Preparation Time: 15 minutes | Cooking Time: 15 minutes | Servings: 2

Ingredients:

- Cherry tomatoes: 2 1/2 cups
- Zucchini, diced: 2 cups
- Bell peppers (various colors), chopped: 2 cups
- Red onions, cut into wedges: 1 1/2 cups
- Mushrooms: 2 cups
- Feta cheese, cubed: 1 cup
- Olive oil: 3 tablespoons
- Balsamic vinegar: 2 tablespoons
- Dried oregano: 2 teaspoons
- Garlic powder: 1 teaspoon
- Salt and black pepper: to taste
- Wooden skewers: soaked in water

For the Feta Dip:
- Feta cheese: 1 cup
- Greek yogurt: 1/2 cup
- Lemon juice: 1 tablespoon
- Fresh parsley, chopped: 1 tablespoon
- Salt and black pepper: to taste

Instructions:

Preparation: soak wooden skewers in water to prevent them from burning while cooking. Preheat the grill or grill pan to medium-high heat.

Vegetable skewers: in a large bowl, mix cherry tomatoes, zucchini, bell peppers, red onions and mushrooms.

In a small bowl, whisk together olive oil, balsamic vinegar, dried oregano, garlic powder, salt and black pepper.

Pour the dressing over the vegetables and toss until well coated.

Thread the marinated vegetables onto the soaked skewers, alternating between different types of vegetables.

Grilling: place skewers on the preheated grill and cook for about 10-12 minutes, turning occasionally, until vegetables are tender and slightly charred.

Feta dip: combine feta cheese, Greek yogurt, lemon juice, chopped parsley, salt and black pepper in a blender or food processor.

Blend until smooth and creamy.

Serve the hot Mediterranean vegetable skewers with the feta dip on the side.

Nutritional Values (per serving): Calories 320 | Fat 20g | Carbohydrates 25g | Protein 12g

66. Smoked Salmon Cucumber Roll

Preparation Time: 15 minutes | Cooking Time: 0 minutes | Servings: 2

Ingredients:

- Smoked salmon: 7 oz
- Cucumber: 1 large
- Cream cheese: 1/2 cup
- Fresh dill, chopped: 1 tablespoon
- Lemon juice: 1 teaspoon
- Salt and pepper: to taste

Instructions:

Wash the cucumber and use a vegetable peeler to slice it lengthwise into thin strips. Pat the cucumber strips dry with a paper towel to remove excess moisture.

In a bowl, mix the cream cheese, fresh dill, lemon juice, salt and pepper. Stir well until all ingredients are evenly incorporated.

Lay out the cucumber strips on a clean surface. Spread a thin layer of the cream cheese mixture over each cucumber strip.

Place a slice of smoked salmon on the cream cheese-covered cucumber strip. Tightly roll up the strip and secure with a toothpick if needed.

Repeat the process for the remaining cucumber strips.

Once all the rolls are prepared, refrigerate them for at least 30 minutes to allow the flavors to meld.

Nutritional Values (per serving): Calories 220 | Fat 15g | Carbohydrates 5g | Protein 18g

67. Crispy Parmesan Zucchini Chips

Preparation Time: 15 minutes | Cooking Time: 20 minutes | Servings: 2

Ingredients:
- Zucchini, thinly sliced: 3 cups
- Grated Parmesan cheese: 1/2 cup
- Almond flour: 1/4 cup
- Garlic powder: 1/2 teaspoon
- Onion powder: 1/2 teaspoon
- Paprika: 1/2 teaspoon
- Dried oregano: 1/2 teaspoon
- Salt and pepper: to taste
- Eggs, beaten: 2 large
- Cooking spray: as needed

Instructions:

Preheat the oven to 200°C (392°F for conventional ovens) and line a baking sheet with parchment paper.

In a shallow bowl, mix almond flour, grated Parmesan, garlic powder, onion powder, paprika, dried oregano, salt and pepper.

Dip each zucchini slice into the beaten eggs, allowing the excess to drip off.

Coat the zucchini slices with the Parmesan mixture, pressing lightly to ensure the coating sticks.

Place the coated zucchini slices in a single layer on the prepared baking sheet.

Lightly spray the zucchini slices with cooking spray to help them crisp up in the oven.

Bake for 15-20 minutes, until the zucchini chips are golden brown and crispy.

Remove from the oven and let cool for a few minutes before serving.

Nutritional Values (per serving): Calories 120 | Fat 8g | Carbohydrates 5g | Protein 7g

68. Buffalo Chicken Lettuce Wraps

Preparation Time: 15 minutes | Cooking Time: 15 minutes | Servings: 4

Ingredients:
- Ground chicken: 1 pound
- Olive oil: 1 tablespoon
- Small onion, finely diced: 1/2 cup
- Garlic cloves, minced: 2 cloves
- Buffalo sauce: 1/2 cup
- Onion powder: 1 teaspoon
- Garlic powder: 1 teaspoon
- Smoked paprika: 1 teaspoon
- Salt and pepper: to taste
- Iceberg lettuce, leaves separated and cleaned: 1 head
- Cherry tomatoes, diced: 2 cups
- Blue cheese, crumbled: 1 cup
- Green onions, thinly sliced: 1/2 cup
- Fresh cilantro: for garnishing

Instructions:
Heat the olive oil in a large skillet over medium heat.

Add the diced onion and minced garlic, sautéing until soft.

Add the ground chicken to the skillet, breaking it apart with a spatula. Cook until the chicken is browned and fully cooked.

Season the chicken with onion powder, garlic powder, smoked paprika, salt and pepper.

Stir in the Buffalo sauce, ensuring the chicken is evenly coated. Simmer for an additional 5 minutes.

While the chicken simmers, prepare the lettuce wraps. Take clean iceberg lettuce leaves and pat them dry.

Spoon the Buffalo chicken mixture onto each lettuce leaf.

Top with diced cherry tomatoes, crumbled blue cheese and sliced green onions, garnishing with fresh cilantro.

Serve immediately and enjoy the delicious low-carb Buffalo Chicken Lettuce Wraps!

Nutritional Values (per serving): Calories 380 | Fat 22g | Carbohydrates 8g | Protein 35g

69. Garlic Herb Edamame

Preparation Time: 10 minutes | Cooking Time: 10 minutes | Servings: 2-4

Ingredients:

- Frozen edamame, unshelled: 14 oz
- Garlic cloves, minced: 3 cloves
- Olive oil: 2 tablespoons
- Dried oregano: 1 teaspoon
- Dried thyme: 1 teaspoon
- Salt: 1/2 teaspoon or to taste
- Black pepper: 1/4 teaspoon or as desired
- Fresh parsley, chopped: 1 tablespoon (for garnish)

Instructions:

Prepare edamame: bring a large pot of water to a boil.

Add the frozen edamame and cook for 5-7 minutes until tender.

Drain the edamame and set aside.

Sauté garlic: heat the olive oil in a large skillet over medium heat.

Add the minced garlic and sauté for 1-2 minutes until fragrant.

Add Edamame: stir the cooked edamame into the skillet with the garlic.

Season with herbs: sprinkle the dried oregano, dried thyme, salt and black pepper over the edamame.

Cook for another 3 to 5 minutes, stirring occasionally, to allow the flavors to meld.

Garnish and serve: remove the skillet from the heat.

Sprinkle fresh parsley over the edamame and gently toss.

Transfer the garlic herb edamame to a serving dish.

Nutritional Values (per serving): Calories: 134 | Fat: 8g | Carbohydrates: 7g | Protein: 3g

70. Mini Caprese Salad Skewers

Preparation Time: 15 minutes | Cooking Time: 0 minutes | Servings: 4

Ingredients:

- Cherry tomatoes: 1 1/2 cups
- Fresh mozzarella cheese, cut into small cubes: 1 1/2 cups
- Fresh basil leaves: 1/2 cup
- Cold-pressed olive oil: 2 tablespoons
- Balsamic glaze: 1 tablespoon
- Salt and pepper: to taste
- Toothpicks or small skewers

Instructions:

Thoroughly wash the cherry tomatoes and basil leaves. Pat dry with a kitchen towel.

Cut the cherry tomatoes into halves.

Thread a half cherry tomato onto a toothpick or small skewer, followed by a cube of mozzarella cheese and a basil leaf. Repeat the process until the toothpick is filled.

Arrange the prepared skewers on a serving platter.

For the dressing: in a small bowl, whisk together the extra virgin olive oil, balsamic glaze, salt and pepper.

Drizzle the dressing over the skewers just before serving.

Nutritional Values (per serving): Calories: 150 | Fat: 10g | Carbohydrates: 5g | Protein: 8g

71. Sesame Ginger Snap Peas

Preparation Time: 10 minutes | Cooking Time: 5 minutes | Servings: 4

Ingredients:

- Snap peas, ends trimmed: 4 cups
- Sesame seeds: 1 tablespoon
- Sesame oil: 1 tablespoon
- Soy sauce: 2 tablespoons
- Fresh ginger, minced: 1 tablespoon
- Garlic cloves, finely chopped: 2 cloves
- Rice vinegar: 1 teaspoon
- Honey (optional, for sweetness): 1 teaspoon
- Olive oil: 1 teaspoon
- Salt and pepper: to taste

Instructions:

Prepare snap peas: wash the snap peas and trim the ends.

Sesame ginger sauce: in a small bowl, whisk together sesame oil, soy sauce, minced ginger, chopped garlic, rice vinegar, honey (if using), olive oil, salt and pepper.

Blanch snap peas: bring a pot of water to a boil. Add the snap peas and cook for 2 minutes. Drain and immediately place them in a bowl of ice water to stop the cooking process. Drain again.

Sauté snap peas: heat a pan over medium heat. Add sesame seeds and toast for 1 to 2 minutes until golden brown. Remove from the pan and set aside.

In the same pan, add the blanched snap peas and the sesame ginger sauce. Sauté for 2 to 3 minutes until the peas are coated and heated through.

Transfer the sesame ginger snap peas to a serving platter.

Sprinkle with toasted sesame seeds.

Nutritional Values (per serving): Calories: 145 | Fat: 6g | Carbohydrates: 7g | Protein: 9g

72. Prosciutto-Wrapped Asparagus Spears

Preparation Time: 15 minutes | Cooking Time: 15 minutes | Servings: 2

Ingredients:

- Fresh asparagus spears, tough ends trimmed: 1/2 pound
- Thinly sliced prosciutto: 3.5 oz
- Olive oil: 1 tablespoon
- Garlic powder: 1 teaspoon
- Salt and pepper: to taste
- Fresh lemon wedges: for serving

Instructions:

Preheat your oven to 200°C (392°F).

Drizzle olive oil over the trimmed asparagus spears.

Sprinkle with garlic powder, salt and pepper, ensuring the asparagus is well coated.

Take a slice of prosciutto and wrap it spirally from bottom to top around each asparagus spear.

Place the wrapped asparagus on a parchment-lined baking sheet.

Bake in the preheated oven for approximately 12-15 minutes, until the prosciutto is crispy and the asparagus is tender.

Remove from the oven and let rest for a minute.

Serve the prosciutto-wrapped asparagus spears with fresh lemon wedges on the side.

Nutritional Values (per serving): Calories: 230 | Fat: 16g | Carbohydrates: 7g | Protein: 15g

73. Tomato Basil Mozzarella Tartlets

Preparation Time: 15 minutes | Cooking Time: 10 minutes | Servings: 4

Ingredients:

- Cherry tomatoes, halved: 2 1/2 cups
- Fresh mozzarella, cubed: 1 3/4 cups
- Fresh basil, finely chopped: 1/4 cup
- Extra-virgin olive oil: 2 tablespoons
- Balsamic glaze: 2 teaspoons
- Salt and pepper: to taste

Instructions:

Preheat the oven to 180°C (350°F).

In a mixing bowl, combine the halved cherry tomatoes, cubed mozzarella and finely chopped fresh basil.

Drizzle the mixture with extra-virgin olive oil and gently toss until the ingredients are well coated.

Season the mixture with salt and pepper to ensure even flavor distribution.

Lightly grease a muffin pan or use silicone muffin cups.

Distribute the tomato-mozzarella-basil mixture evenly among the muffin cups.

Bake in the preheated oven for 10 minutes, until the mozzarella has melted and the tomatoes are slightly roasted.

Remove from the oven and let cool for a few minutes.

Drizzle each tartlet with balsamic glaze just before serving.

Nutritional Values (per serving):
Calories: 220 | Fat: 15g | Carbohydrates: 8g | Protein: 12g

74. Eggplant Pizza Bites: Low-Carb and Flavorful

Preparation Time: 15 minutes | Cooking Time: 20 minutes | Servings: 4

Ingredients:
- Eggplant, sliced into thin rounds: 4 cups
- Cherry tomatoes, halved: 1 1/2 cups
- Mozzarella cheese, shredded: 1 1/2 cups
- Parmesan cheese, grated: 1/2 cup
- Low-carb pizza sauce: 1/2 cup
- Olive oil: 1 tablespoon
- Dried oregano: 1 teaspoon
- Garlic powder: 1 teaspoon
- Salt and pepper: to taste
- Fresh basil leaves: for garnish

Instructions:
Preheat the oven to 200°C (400°F).

Place the eggplant slices on a kitchen towel and sprinkle with salt. Let sit for 10 minutes to draw out excess moisture. Pat dry with another paper towel.

Arrange the eggplant slices on a baking sheet. Brush each slice with olive oil and sprinkle with garlic powder.

Bake in the preheated oven for 10 minutes or until slightly softened.

Remove the eggplant from the oven and spread a thin layer of low-carb pizza sauce on each slice.

Top the eggplant slices with halved cherry tomatoes, shredded mozzarella and grated Parmesan.

Sprinkle dried oregano, salt and pepper over the toppings.

Return the baking sheet to the oven and bake for an additional 10 minutes, until the cheese is melted and bubbly.

Garnish with fresh basil leaves before serving.

Nutritional Values (per serving):
Calories: 215 | Fat: 15g | Carbohydrates: 10g | Protein: 12g

75. Spiced Turkey Jerky

Preparation Time: 20 minutes | Dehydration Time: 2-3 hours | Servings: 4

Ingredients:
- Turkey breast, sliced thinly: 1 pound
- Soy sauce: 2 tablespoons
- Worcestershire sauce: 1 tablespoon
- Garlic powder: 1 teaspoon
- Onion powder: 1 teaspoon
- Smoked paprika: 1 teaspoon
- Cayenne pepper: 1/2 teaspoon
- Black pepper: 1/2 teaspoon
- Cinnamon: 1/4 teaspoon
- Cumin: 1/4 teaspoon
- Olive oil: 1 tablespoon

Instructions:

Marinate the turkey: in a mixing bowl, combine the soy sauce, Worcestershire sauce, garlic powder, onion powder, smoked paprika, cayenne pepper, black pepper, cinnamon, cumin and olive oil to create a marinade.

Place the thinly sliced turkey breast into a resealable plastic bag or a shallow dish. Pour the marinade over the turkey, ensuring each piece is thoroughly coated. Seal the bag or cover the dish and let it marinate in the refrigerator for at least 2 hours or overnight to intensify the flavors.

Prepare for dehydrating: preheat your oven to its lowest setting, around 71-77°C (160-170°F) or prepare a food dehydrator set to 71°C (160°F).

Arrange the turkey: remove the turkey slices from the marinade, allowing the excess to drip off. Place the slices on oven racks or dehydrator trays, making sure they do not overlap to allow for proper air circulation.

Dehydrator method: place the turkey in the oven, leaving the door slightly ajar to allow moisture to escape. Dry for 2 to 3 hours or until the turkey achieves a jerky-like consistency.

Dehydrator method: dry at 71°C (160°F) for 2 to 3 hours, checking periodically until the turkey is dry and leathery, but not brittle.

Cool and store: allow the jerky to cool completely before transferring it to an airtight container for storage.

Nutritional Value (per serving): Calories: 120 | Fat: 3g | Carbohydrates: 2g | Protein: 22g

76. Stuffed Mushrooms with Spinach and Artichokes

Preparation Time: 20 minutes | Cooking Time: 25 minutes | Servings: 4

Ingredients:

- Large mushrooms, cleaned and stems removed: 1 pound
- Fresh spinach, chopped: 2 cups
- Artichoke hearts, drained and diced: 1 cup
- Cream cheese, softened: 7 oz
- Parmesan cheese, grated: 1/2 cup
- Garlic cloves, chopped: 2 cloves
- Olive oil: 1 tablespoon
- Dried oregano: 1 teaspoon
- Salt and pepper: to taste

Instructions:

Preheat the oven to 180°C (350°F).

In a pan over medium heat, sauté the chopped spinach in olive oil until wilted. Add the chopped garlic and cook for another 2 minutes. Remove from heat.

In a mixing bowl, combine cream cheese, diced artichoke hearts, Parmesan, dried oregano, sautéed spinach, salt and pepper. Mix well until all ingredients are evenly incorporated.

Fill each mushroom cap with the spinach-artichoke mixture, pressing down lightly.

Place the stuffed mushrooms on a baking sheet and bake in the preheated oven for 20-25 minutes or until the mushrooms are tender.

Remove from the oven and let cool for a few minutes before serving.

Nutritional Information (per serving): Calories 220 | Fat 15g | Carbohydrates 10g | Protein 12g

77. Goat Cheese Balls with Pistachio Crust

Preparation Time: 15 minutes | Cooking Time: 10 minutes | Servings: 2

Ingredients:

- Goat cheese: 7 oz
- Pistachios, shelled and finely chopped: 1 cup
- Almond flour: 2 tablespoons
- Dried thyme: 1 teaspoon
- Black pepper: 1/2 teaspoon
- Egg: 1 large
- Parmesan cheese, grated: 1/2 cup
- Olive oil: for frying

Instructions:

In a bowl, mix together the goat cheese, almond flour, dried thyme and black pepper until well combined.

Form the mixture into small balls, about 2.5 cm in diameter.

In a separate bowl, whisk the egg. In another bowl, mix the finely chopped pistachios and grated Parmesan cheese.

Dip each goat cheese ball into the beaten egg, ensuring it is fully coated. Then roll the ball in the pistachio-Parmesan mixture, pressing lightly so the coating sticks.

Heat olive oil in a pan over medium heat. Fry the coated goat cheese balls until they are golden brown and crispy, about 2-3 minutes per side.

Remove the goat cheese balls from the pan and place them on a paper towel to absorb any excess oil.

Serve the warm goat cheese balls with pistachio crust and enjoy!

Nutritional Information (per serving): Calories 280 | Fat 22g | Carbohydrates 6g | Protein 14g

78. Baked Parmesan Chips

Preparation Time: 10 minutes | Cooking Time: 10 minutes | Servings: 4

Ingredients:

- Parmesan cheese, finely grated: 2 cups
- Garlic powder: 1 teaspoon
- Dried oregano: 1 teaspoon
- Dried basil: 1 teaspoon
- Black pepper, freshly ground: 1/2 teaspoon

Instructions:

Preheat the oven to 180°C (350°F).

In a bowl, mix together the finely grated Parmesan cheese, garlic powder, dried oregano, dried basil and freshly ground black pepper. Ensure the spices are evenly distributed.

Line a baking sheet with parchment paper.

Using a tablespoon, drop small heaps of the Parmesan mixture onto the prepared baking sheet, spacing them about 5 cm apart. Gently flatten the heaps with the back of the spoon to form thin circles.

Bake in the preheated oven for 8-10 minutes, until the edges are golden brown and the chips feel firm.

Remove from the oven and let the Parmesan chips cool on the baking sheet for a few minutes to firm up.

Once cooled, gently transfer the chips to a wire rack and let them cool completely.

Serve as a crispy snack or alongside your favorite dip.

Nutritional Information (per serving): Calories 120 | Fat 9g | Carbohydrates 1g | Protein 10g

79. Cucumber Sushi Rolls with Smoked Salmon

Preparation Time: 20 minutes | Cooking Time: 0 minutes | Servings: 2

Ingredients:

- Cucumber, cut into julienne strips: 1 1/2 cups
- Smoked salmon: 5 oz
- Cream cheese: 1/2 cup
- Avocado, sliced: 1/4 cup
- Chives, finely chopped: 1 tablespoon
- Sesame seeds: 1 teaspoon
- Nori sheets (seaweed): 2 sheets

Instructions:

Lay a nori sheet on a clean surface.

Spread a thin layer of cream cheese evenly across the nori sheet.

Place half of the sliced cucumber on the lower third of the nori sheet.

Layer half of the smoked salmon over the cucumber.

Add half of the avocado slices on top of the salmon.

Sprinkle half of the chives and sesame seeds over the avocado.

Carefully roll the nori from the bottom up, using a bamboo mat if available, to form a tight roll.

Repeat the process with the second nori sheet and the remaining ingredients.

Once both rolls are completed, use a sharp knife to cut each roll into bite-sized pieces.

Arrange the cucumber sushi rolls on a serving platter.

Nutritional Information (per serving):
Calories 280 | Fat 18g | Carbohydrates 8g | Protein 20g

80. Greek Yogurt and Berry Parfait

Preparation Time: 15 minutes | Cooking Time: 0 minutes | Servings: 2

Ingredients:

- Greek yogurt: 1 1/4 cups
- Mixed berries (strawberries, blueberries, raspberries): 1 cup
- Almond slivers: 1/4 cup
- Chia seeds: 2 tablespoons
- Unsweetened coconut flakes: 2 tablespoons
- Vanilla extract: 1 teaspoon
- Sugar-free sweetener (optional): 1 tablespoon

Instructions:

In a bowl, mix Greek yogurt with vanilla extract and sugar-free sweetener (if using). Stir until well combined.

Layer half of the Greek yogurt mixture evenly into glasses or bowls.

Add a layer of mixed berries over the yogurt.

Sprinkle almond slivers, chia seeds and coconut flakes over the berries.

Repeat the layers until the glasses are filled, finishing with a layer of berries topped with a sprinkling of almonds, chia seeds and coconut flakes.

Refrigerate for at least 30 minutes to allow the flavors to meld together.

Serve chilled and enjoy your delicious low-carb Greek yogurt and berry parfait!

Nutritional Information (per serving): Calories 250 | Fat 15g | Carbohydrates 20g | Protein 12g

Chapter 8: Dessert

81. Peanut Butter Energy Bars with Protein Filling

Preparation Time: 15 minutes | Cooking Time: 25 minutes | Servings: 4

Ingredients:

- Natural peanut butter: 3/4 cup
- Almond flour: 1 cup
- Protein powder (vanilla or chocolate flavor): 1/2 cup
- Chia seeds: 2 tablespoons
- Unsweetened coconut flakes: 1/4 cup
- Sugar-free maple syrup: 1/4 cup
- Vanilla extract: 1 teaspoon
- Salt: a pinch

Instructions:

Preheat the oven to 180°C (350°F) and line a baking dish with parchment paper.

In a mixing bowl, combine natural peanut butter, almond flour, protein powder, chia seeds, coconut flakes, sugar-free maple syrup, vanilla extract and a pinch of salt. Mix until well combined.

Firmly press the mixture into the prepared baking dish, creating an even layer.

Bake in the preheated oven for 20-25 minutes or until the edges turn golden brown.

Remove from the oven and let the mixture cool completely in the dish before cutting into bars.

Once cooled, cut into bars and store in an airtight container for up to one week.

Nutritional Information (per serving):
Calories: 213 | Fat: 12g | Carbohydrates: 10g | Protein: 15g

82. Keto-Friendly Chocolate Almond Bliss Bars

Preparation Time: 15 minutes | Cooking Time: 30 minutes | Servings: 2

Ingredients:

- Almond flour: 1 1/2 cups
- Unsweetened cocoa powder: 1/2 cup
- Almond butter: 1/3 cup
- Coconut oil, melted: 1/4 cup
- Powdered erythritol: 1/4 cup
- Vanilla extract: 1 teaspoon
- Chopped almonds: 1/2 cup
- Salt: a pinch

Instructions:

Preheat the oven to 180°C (350°F) and line a baking dish with parchment paper.

In a large mixing bowl, combine almond flour, cocoa powder, powdered erythritol, chopped almonds and a pinch of salt.

In a separate bowl, mix almond butter, melted coconut oil and vanilla extract until well combined.

Add the wet ingredients to the dry ingredients and stir until a thick dough forms.

Press the dough evenly into the prepared baking dish.

Bake in the preheated oven for 25-30 minutes or until the edges are set.

Allow the bars to cool completely before cutting into squares.

Nutritional Information (per serving):
Calories: 250 | Fat: 20g | Carbohydrates: 8g | Protein: 6g

83. Low-Carb Blueberry Chia Seed Muffins

Preparation Time: 15 minutes | Cooking Time: 25 minutes | Servings: 4

Ingredients:

- Almond flour: 1 1/2 cups
- Coconut flour: 1/4 cup
- Chia seeds: 1 tablespoon
- Baking powder: 1 teaspoon
- Baking soda: 1/2 teaspoon
- Salt: 1/4 teaspoon
- Eggs: 2 large
- Unsweetened almond milk: 1/2 cup
- Melted coconut oil: 1/3 cup
- Vanilla extract: 1 teaspoon
- Fresh blueberries: 1 cup

Instructions:

Preheat the oven to 180°C (350°F) and line a muffin tray with paper liners.

In a large mixing bowl, combine almond flour, coconut flour, chia seeds, baking powder, baking soda and salt. Mix well.

In another bowl, whisk together eggs, almond milk, melted coconut oil and vanilla extract.

Add the wet ingredients to the dry ingredients and stir until well combined.

Gently fold in the fresh blueberries.

Evenly distribute the batter among the muffin cups, filling each about 2/3 full.

Bake in the preheated oven for 20-25 minutes or until a toothpick inserted in the center comes out clean.

Let the muffins cool in the pan for 5 minutes, then transfer to a wire rack to cool completely.

Nutritional Information (per serving): **Calories: 220 | Fat: 18g | Carbohydrates: 8g | Protein: 7g**

84. No-Bake Coconut Cashew Energy Bites

Preparation Time: 15 minutes | Cooking Time: 0 minutes | Servings: 12 bites

Ingredients:
- Cashew nuts: 1 cup
- Unsweetened shredded coconut: 1/2 cup
- Almond flour: 1/4 cup
- Chia seeds: 2 tablespoons
- Sugar-free maple syrup: 1/4 cup
- Vanilla extract: 1 teaspoon
- Salt: 1/4 teaspoon
- Coconut oil, melted: 2 tablespoons

Instructions:

Combine cashews, shredded coconut, almond flour and chia seeds in a food processor. Pulse until the mixture reaches a coarse texture.

Add sugar-free maple syrup, vanilla extract, salt and melted coconut oil to the food processor. Blend until the mixture forms a sticky dough.

Using your hands, roll the dough into bite-sized balls, about 1 inch in diameter.

Place the energy balls on a baking sheet lined with parchment paper and refrigerate for at least 30 minutes to set.

Once chilled, transfer the energy bites to an airtight container and store in the refrigerator.

Nutritional Information (per serving): **Calories: 120 | Fat: 9g | Carbohydrates: 6g | Protein: 3g**

85. Almond Flour Banana Nut Muffins

Preparation Time: 15 minutes | Baking Time: 25 minutes | Servings: 12 muffins

Ingredients:
- Almond flour: 2 cups
- Coconut flour: 1/2 cup
- Baking powder: 1 1/2 teaspoons

- Baking soda: 1/2 teaspoon
- Salt: 1/4 teaspoon
- Ripe bananas, mashed: 1 1/4 cups
- Eggs: 3 large
- Unsalted butter, melted: 1/4 cup
- Unsweetened almond milk: 1/4 cup
- Vanilla extract: 1 teaspoon
- Chopped walnuts or pecans: 1 cup

Instructions:

Preheat the oven to 180°C (350°F) and line a muffin tin with paper liners.

In a large bowl, mix together almond flour, coconut flour, baking powder, baking soda and salt. Ensure everything is well combined for a uniform mixture.

In a separate bowl, whisk together the mashed bananas, eggs, melted butter, almond milk and vanilla extract until smooth.

Combine the wet ingredients with the dry ingredients and stir until well incorporated. Fold in the chopped nuts.

Distribute the batter evenly among the muffin cups, filling each about 2/3 full.

Bake in the preheated oven for 20-25 minutes or until a toothpick inserted into the center comes out clean.

Allow the muffins to cool in the pan for 5 minutes, then transfer to a wire rack to cool completely.

Nutritional Information (per serving):
Calories: 220 | Fat: 16g | Carbohydrates: 14g | Protein: 7g

86. Cinnamon Roll Protein Bars for Low-Carb Delights

Preparation Time: 15 minutes | Baking Time: 25 minutes | Servings: 4 bars

Ingredients:

- Almond flour: 2 cups
- Whey protein powder: 1/4 cup
- Coconut flour: 1/4 cup
- Ground flaxseeds: 1 tablespoon
- Baking powder: 1 teaspoon
- Cinnamon: 1/2 teaspoon
- Salt: 1/4 teaspoon
- Unsweetened almond butter: 1/2 cup
- Coconut oil, melted: 1/4 cup
- Eggs: 2 large
- Vanilla extract: 1 teaspoon
- Erythritol (or low-carb sweetener of choice): 2 tablespoons
- Unsweetened almond milk: 1/4 cup

Instructions:

Preheat the oven to 180°C (350°F) and line a baking dish with parchment paper.

In a large bowl, whisk together almond flour, whey protein powder, coconut flour, ground flaxseeds, baking powder, cinnamon and salt.

In a separate bowl, mix together almond butter, melted coconut oil, eggs, vanilla extract and erythritol until well combined.

Add the wet ingredients to the dry ingredients and stir until a dough forms. If the dough is too dry, add almond milk by the tablespoon until it reaches a smooth consistency.

Press the dough evenly into the prepared baking dish and smooth the surface with a spatula.

Bake for 20-25 minutes or until the edges are golden brown and a toothpick inserted into the center comes out clean.

Allow the bars to cool completely in the dish before cutting into 4 equal portions.

Nutritional Information (per serving):
Calories: 320 | Fat: 25g | Carbohydrates: 8g | Protein: 15g

87. Dark Chocolate Avocado Keto Brownies

Preparation Time: 15 minutes | Cooking Time: 25 minutes | Servings: 4

Ingredients:
- Dark chocolate (at least 70% cocoa), chopped: 7 oz
- Ripe avocado, pureed: 2/3 cup
- Almond flour: 1 cup
- Unsweetened cocoa powder: 1/2 cup
- Unsalted butter, melted: 1/2 cup
- Eggs: 4 large
- Erythritol (or a keto-friendly sweetener of your choice): 3/4 cup
- Vanilla extract: 1 teaspoon
- Baking powder: 1/2 teaspoon
- Salt: a pinch

Instructions:
Preheat the oven to 180°C (350°F) and grease a square baking pan (8x8 inches) with butter or line it with parchment paper.

Melt the dark chocolate in a heatproof bowl over a water bath or in the microwave in 30-second intervals, stirring until smooth. Allow to cool slightly.

In a large mixing bowl, combine the pureed avocado, melted butter, eggs and vanilla extract. Stir until well mixed.

In a separate bowl, whisk together almond flour, cocoa powder, erythritol, baking powder and a pinch of salt.

Gradually add the dry ingredients to the wet ingredients, stirring constantly to avoid lumps.

Add the melted chocolate and stir until the batter is smooth and well incorporated.

Pour the batter into the prepared baking pan, spreading it evenly.

Bake in the preheated oven for about 25 minutes or until a toothpick inserted in the center comes out with moist crumbs, but not wet.

Allow the brownies to cool in the pan for at least 15 minutes before transferring to a wire rack to cool completely.

Nutritional Information (per serving):
Calories: 320 | Fat: 28g | Carbohydrates: 10g | Protein: 8g

88. Lemon Poppy Seed Almond Flour Snack Bars

Preparation Time: 15 minutes | Cooking Time: 25 minutes | Servings: 4

Ingredients:
- Almond flour: 2 cups
- Coconut flour: 1/2 cup
- Baking powder: 1/2 teaspoon
- Salt: 1/4 teaspoon
- Eggs: 3 large
- Unsweetened almond milk: 1/3 cup
- Melted coconut oil: 1/4 cup
- Vanilla extract: 1 teaspoon
- Zest of 1 lemon
- Lemon juice: 2 tablespoons
- Poppy seeds: 2 tablespoons
- Powdered erythritol (or sweetener of choice): 1/3 cup

Instructions:
Preheat the oven to 180°C (350°F) and grease a square baking pan (8x8 inches) with coconut oil.

In a large mixing bowl, combine almond flour, coconut flour, baking powder and salt.

In another bowl, whisk together eggs, almond milk, melted coconut oil, vanilla extract, lemon zest and lemon juice.

Add the wet ingredients to the dry ingredients and stir until well combined.

Fold in the poppy seeds and erythritol powder.

Pour the batter into the prepared baking pan, spreading it evenly.

Bake for 25 minutes or until the edges are golden brown and a toothpick inserted in the center comes out clean.

Allow the bars to cool completely before cutting them into 4 equal portions.

Nutritional Information (per serving):
Calories: 250 | Fat: 20g | Carbohydrates: 8g | Protein: 9g

89. Hazelnut Espresso Energy Bites

Preparation Time: 15 minutes | Cooking Time: 0 minutes | Servings: 2

Ingredients:

- Hazelnuts: 3/4 cup

- Almond flour: 1/2 cup

- Unsweetened coconut flakes: 1/3 cup

- Ground flaxseed: 2 tablespoons

- Chia seeds: 1 tablespoon

- Cocoa powder: 2 tablespoons

- Instant espresso powder: 1 tablespoon

- Coconut oil, melted: 2 tablespoons

- Vanilla extract: 1 teaspoon

- Sugar-free maple syrup: 2-3 tablespoons

Instructions:

Finely grind the hazelnuts in a food processor.

Add almond flour, coconut flakes, ground flaxseed, chia seeds, cocoa powder and instant espresso powder to the hazelnuts. Pulse until well combined.

In a separate bowl, mix melted coconut oil, vanilla extract and sugar-free maple syrup.

Add the wet ingredients to the dry ingredients in the food processor. Pulse until a sticky dough forms.

Take small portions of the dough and roll them into bite-sized balls.

Place the energy bites on a parchment-lined tray and refrigerate for at least 30 minutes to set.

Enjoy as a quick energy boost!

Nutritional Information (per serving):
Calories: 120 | Fat: 10g | Carbohydrates: 5g | Protein: 3g

90. Low-Carb Pumpkin Spice Muffins

Preparation Time: 15 minutes | Cooking Time: 25 minutes | Servings: 4

Ingredients:

- Almond flour: 2 cups

- Coconut flour: 1/2 cup

- Baking powder: 1 teaspoon

- Baking soda: 1/2 teaspoon

- Salt: 1/2 teaspoon

- Pumpkin spice mix: 2 teaspoons

- Eggs: 4 large

- Pumpkin puree: 2/3 cup

- Unsalted butter, melted: 1/2 cup

- Erythritol (or a low-carb sweetener of your choice): 1/2 cup

- Vanilla extract: 1 teaspoon

- Chopped walnuts (optional): 1/2 cup

Instructions:

Preheat the oven to 180°C (350°F) and line a muffin tin with paper liners.

In a large bowl, mix together almond flour, coconut flour, baking powder, baking soda, salt and pumpkin spice mix.

In another bowl, whisk together eggs, pumpkin puree, melted butter, erythritol and vanilla extract until well combined.

Add the wet ingredients to the dry ingredients and stir until well combined. If desired, fold in the chopped walnuts.

Spoon the batter into the prepared muffin tin, filling each cup about 2/3 full.

Bake in the preheated oven for 20-25 minutes or until a toothpick inserted in the center comes out clean.

Let the muffins cool in the tin for 5 minutes before transferring them to a wire rack to cool completely.

Nutritional Information (per serving):
Calories: 320 | Fat: 25g | Carbohydrates: 10g | Protein: 12g

91. Walnut-Cranberry Keto Granola Bars

Preparation Time: 15 minutes | Cooking Time: 25 minutes | Servings: 4

Ingredients:
- Walnuts, chopped: 1 1/2 cups
- Almonds, chopped: 1 cup
- Unsweetened coconut flakes: 1/2 cup
- Chia seeds: 2 tablespoons
- Flaxseeds: 2 tablespoons
- Pumpkin seeds: 1/2 cup
- Unsweetened dried cranberries: 1/3 cup
- Cinnamon: 1 teaspoon
- Salt: 1/2 teaspoon
- Coconut oil, melted: 2 tablespoons
- Almond butter: 2 tablespoons
- Sugar-free maple syrup: 2 tablespoons
- Vanilla extract: 1 teaspoon
- Eggs: 2 large

Instructions:
Preheat the oven to 160°C (320°F) and line a baking dish with parchment paper.

In a large mixing bowl, combine chopped walnuts, almond slices, coconut flakes, chia seeds, flaxseeds, pumpkin seeds, dried cranberries, cinnamon and salt.

In a separate bowl, whisk together melted coconut oil, almond butter, sugar-free maple syrup, vanilla extract and eggs.

Add the wet ingredients to the dry ingredients and stir until well combined.

Transfer the mixture to the prepared baking dish and press down firmly to create a compact layer.

Bake in the preheated oven for 25 minutes or until the edges are golden brown.

Allow the granola bars to cool completely in the dish before cutting them into bars.

Nutritional Information (per serving):
Calories: 280 | Fat: 24g |
Carbohydrates: 9g | Protein: 7g

92. Vanilla Almond Chia Pudding Cups

Preparation Time: 10 minutes | Chill Time: 4 hours | Servings: 2

Ingredients:

- Chia seeds: 1/4 cup

- Almond milk: 1 2/3 cups

- Vanilla extract: 2 teaspoons

- Almonds, chopped: 2 tablespoons

- Unsweetened coconut flakes: 1 tablespoon

- Low-carb sweetener (e.g., erythritol): 1 tablespoon

- Salt: a pinch

Instructions:

In a bowl, combine chia seeds, almond milk, vanilla extract, chopped almonds, coconut flakes, low-carb sweetener and a pinch of salt.

Mix well, ensuring the chia seeds are evenly distributed. Let the mixture sit for 5 minutes, then stir again to prevent clumping.

Cover the bowl and refrigerate for at least 4 hours or overnight. The chia seeds will absorb the liquid and thicken into a pudding-like consistency.

After chilling, stir the mixture well to break up any clumps. Adjust sweetness if necessary.

Divide the chia pudding into individual serving bowls.

Garnish with additional slivered almonds and coconut flakes.

Serve chilled and enjoy the delightful Vanilla Almond Chia Pudding Cups!

Nutritional Information (per serving):
Calories: 250 | Fat: 15g |
Carbohydrates: 20g | Protein: 7g

93. Chocolate Hazelnut Protein Balls

Preparation Time: 15 minutes | Cook Time: 0 minutes | Servings: 2

Ingredients:

- Hazelnuts: 3/4 cup

- Almond flour: 1/4 cup

- Unsweetened cocoa powder: 1/4 cup

- Whey protein powder: 1/4 cup

- Sugar-free chocolate chips: 1/4 cup

- Coconut oil, melted: 2 tablespoons

- Vanilla extract: 1 teaspoon

- Salt: a pinch

- Powdered erythritol (or a low-carb sweetener of your choice): 1/4 cup
- Additional cocoa powder or coconut flakes for rolling (optional)

Instructions:

In a food processor, blend hazelnuts, almond flour, cocoa powder, whey protein powder and a pinch of salt until you achieve a fine, crumbly texture.

Add the sugar-free chocolate chips to the food processor and pulse a few times until they're incorporated into the mixture.

In a separate bowl, whisk together the melted coconut oil and vanilla extract.

With the food processor running, slowly add the coconut oil-vanilla mixture to the dry ingredients. Process until the mixture forms a sticky dough.

Taste the dough and adjust sweetness by adding powdered erythritol (or your preferred low-carb sweetener) if needed. Pulse to combine.

Scoop tablespoon-sized portions of the dough and roll them into balls with your hands. If desired, roll the balls in additional cocoa powder or coconut flakes to coat them.

Place the chocolate hazelnut protein balls on a parchment-lined tray and refrigerate for at least 30 minutes to set.

Enjoy these energy-packed, keto-friendly treats as a snack or dessert!

Nutritional Information (per serving):
Calories: 180 | Fat: 14g | Carbohydrates: 7g | Protein: 8g

94. Low-Carb Zucchini Walnut Muffins

Preparation Time: 15 minutes | Cook Time: 25 minutes | Servings: 4

Ingredients:
- Almond flour: 2 cups
- Coconut flour: 1 cup
- Baking powder: 2 teaspoons
- Ground cinnamon: 2 teaspoons
- Salt: 1/2 teaspoon
- Eggs: 4 large
- Unsweetened almond milk: 2/3 cup
- Melted butter: 1/2 cup
- Vanilla extract: 2 teaspoons
- Grated zucchini: 2 1/2 cups
- Chopped walnuts: 1 1/2 cups

Instructions:
Preheat the oven to 180°C (350°F) and line a muffin tray with paper liners.

In a large mixing bowl, combine almond flour, coconut flour, baking powder, ground cinnamon and salt.

In another bowl, whisk together eggs, almond milk, melted butter and vanilla extract.

Add the wet ingredients to the dry ingredients and stir until well combined.

Fold in the grated zucchini and chopped walnuts until they are evenly distributed throughout the batter.

Spoon the batter into the muffin cups, filling each about two-thirds full.

Bake in the preheated oven for 20-25 minutes or until a toothpick inserted into the center of a muffin comes out clean.

Allow the muffins to cool in the tray for 5 minutes before transferring them to a wire rack to cool completely.

Nutritional Information (per serving):
Calories: 320 | Fat: 25g | Carbohydrates: 10g | Protein: 12g

95. Coconut Macaroon Energy Bars

Preparation Time: 15 minutes | Cooking Time: 20 minutes | Servings: 4

Ingredients:
- Shredded, unsweetened coconut: 1 1/2 cups
- Almond flour: 3/4 cup
- Coconut oil, melted: 1/4 cup
- Powdered erythritol (or low-carb sweetener of choice): 1/4 cup
- Eggs: 2 large
- Vanilla extract: 1 teaspoon
- Salt: a pinch

Instructions:
Preheat the oven to 160°C (320°F) and line a square baking pan with parchment paper.

In a mixing bowl, combine the coconut flakes, almond flour, melted coconut oil, erythritol, eggs, vanilla extract and a pinch of salt. Mix well until a sticky dough forms.

Press the dough evenly into the prepared baking pan, smoothing the surface with a spatula.

Bake in the preheated oven for 20 minutes or until the edges are golden brown.

Remove from the oven and let cool in the pan for 10 minutes.

Lift the parchment paper to transfer the entire slab onto a cutting board. Allow to cool completely before cutting into bars.

Cut into 4 bars after cooling.

Nutritional Information (per serving):
Calories: 230 | Fat: 20g | Carbohydrates: 6g | Protein: 5g

96. Maple Pecan Keto Blondies

Preparation Time: 15 minutes | Cooking Time: 25 minutes | Servings: 12

Ingredients:

- Almond flour: 2 cups
- Unsalted butter, melted: 2/3 cup
- Erythritol (or preferred keto-friendly sweetener): 1/2 cup
- Eggs: 2 large
- Vanilla extract: 1 teaspoon
- Baking powder: 1/2 teaspoon
- Salt: 1/4 teaspoon
- Chopped pecans: 1 cup
- Sugar-free maple syrup: 3 tablespoons

Instructions:

Preheat the oven to 175°C (350°F). Grease a square baking dish (about 8x8 inches) and line it with parchment paper, leaving some overhang for easy removal.

In a large mixing bowl, combine almond flour, melted butter, erythritol, eggs, vanilla extract, baking powder and salt. Mix until a thick batter forms.

Fold in the chopped pecans, ensuring they are evenly distributed throughout the batter.

Pour the batter into the prepared baking dish, spreading it evenly with a spatula.

Drizzle the sugar-free maple syrup over the batter, using a toothpick or knife to create a swirling pattern.

Bake in the preheated oven for 25 minutes, until the edges are golden brown and a toothpick inserted into the center comes out clean.

Allow the blondies to cool in the pan for 10 minutes, then lift them out using the parchment paper overhang and let cool completely on a wire rack.

Nutritional Information (per serving):
Calories: 220 | Fat: 20g | Carbohydrates: 4g | Protein: 5g

97. Raspberry Almond Butter Protein Squares

Preparation Time: 15 minutes | Cooking Time: 25 minutes | Servings: 2

Ingredients:

- Almond flour: 1 1/2 cups
- Whey protein powder (vanilla flavored): 1/2 cup
- Coconut flour: 1/4 cup
- Unsweetened almond butter: 1/2 cup
- Unsalted butter, melted: 1/3 cup
- Powdered erythritol (or other low-carb sweetener): 1/4 cup
- Vanilla extract: 1 teaspoon
- Almond extract: 1/2 teaspoon
- Salt: 1/4 teaspoon
- Fresh raspberries: 1 cup

Instructions:

Preheat the oven to 180°C (350°F) and line a square baking pan (20x20 cm) with parchment paper.

In a large bowl, mix together the almond flour, whey protein powder, coconut flour, powdered erythritol and salt.

In a separate microwave-safe bowl, melt the almond butter and unsalted butter together. Stir until well combined.

Add the melted butter mixture, vanilla extract and almond extract to the dry ingredients. Mix until a thick batter forms.

Gently fold in the fresh raspberries, taking care not to crush them completely.

Press the batter evenly into the prepared baking pan.

Bake in the preheated oven for 25 minutes, until the edges are golden brown.

Allow the squares to cool completely in the pan before cutting them into 16 squares.

Nutritional Information (per serving):

Calories: 230 | Fat: 18g | Carbohydrates: 6g | Protein: 12g

98. Spicy Parmesan Herb Fat Bombs

Preparation Time: 10 minutes | Cooking Time: 15 minutes | Servings: 2

Ingredients:

- Cream cheese, softened: 7 oz
- Unsalted butter, softened: 7 oz
- Parmesan cheese, grated: 1 cup
- Garlic cloves, chopped: 2 cloves
- Fresh parsley, chopped: 1 tablespoon
- Fresh chives, chopped: 1 tablespoon
- Dried oregano: 1 teaspoon
- Black pepper: 1/2 teaspoon
- Salt: 1/4 teaspoon

Instructions:

In a mixing bowl, stir together the softened cream cheese and butter until smooth.

Add the grated Parmesan cheese, chopped garlic, fresh parsley, fresh chives, dried oregano, black pepper and salt to the bowl. Mix well until all ingredients are evenly incorporated.

Transfer the mixture onto a sheet of parchment paper and shape it into a log or desired shape.

Tightly wrap the log in parchment paper and refrigerate for at least 2 hours or until firm.

Preheat the oven to 180°C (350°F).

Unwrap the chilled log and slice it into 1 cm thick slices.

Place the slices on a parchment-lined baking sheet.

Bake for 12-15 minutes or until the edges are golden brown.

Allow the fat bombs to cool completely before serving.

Nutritional Information (per serving):
Calories: 220 | Fat: 20g | Carbohydrates: 2g | Protein: 6g

99. Flourless Cherry Almond Energy Cookies

Preparation Time: 15 minutes | Cooking Time: 12 minutes | Servings: 4

Ingredients:
- Almond flour: 1 1/2 cups
- Unsalted butter, melted: 1/4 cup
- Egg: 1 large
- Erythritol (or your preferred low-carb sweetener): 1/3 cup
- Almond extract: 1 teaspoon
- Baking powder: 1/2 teaspoon
- Salt: 1/4 teaspoon
- Chopped almonds: 1/2 cup
- Unsweetened dried cherries: 1/3 cup

Instructions:
Preheat the oven to 180°C (350°F) and line a baking sheet with parchment paper.

In a mixing bowl, combine almond flour, melted butter, egg, erythritol, almond extract, baking powder and salt. Stir well until a dough forms.

Fold in the chopped almonds and dried cherries until evenly distributed throughout the dough.

Divide the dough into 12 equal portions, shape each portion into a cookie and place on the prepared baking sheet.

Gently flatten each cookie with the back of a spoon or your fingers.

Bake in the preheated oven for 10-12 minutes or until the edges are golden brown.

Allow the cookies to cool on the baking sheet for 5 minutes before transferring them to a wire rack to cool completely.

Nutritional Information (per serving):
Calories: 210 | Fat: 18g | Carbohydrates: 6g | Protein: 7g

100. Matcha Green Tea Protein Muffins

Preparation Time: 15 minutes | Cooking Time: 20 minutes | Servings: 4

Ingredients:
- Almond flour: 1 cup
- Coconut flour: 1/4 cup
- Vanilla protein powder: 2 tablespoons
- Matcha green tea powder: 1 tablespoon
- Baking powder: 1 teaspoon
- Eggs: 3 large
- Unsweetened almond milk: 1/3 cup

- Melted coconut oil: 1/4 cup
- Greek yogurt: 1/4 cup
- Vanilla extract: 1 teaspoon
- Erythritol (or low-carb sweetener of choice): 1/4 cup
- Salt: a pinch

Instructions:

Preheat the oven to 180°C (350°F) and line a muffin tray with paper liners.

In a large mixing bowl, combine almond flour, coconut flour, vanilla protein powder, Matcha green tea powder, baking powder and a pinch of salt.

In a separate bowl, whisk together eggs, unsweetened almond milk, melted coconut oil, Greek yogurt, vanilla extract and erythritol until smooth.

Gradually add the wet ingredients to the dry ingredients, stirring until well combined.

Distribute the batter evenly among the muffin cups.

Bake in the preheated oven for 18-20 minutes or until a toothpick inserted into the center comes out clean.

Allow the muffins to cool in the tray for 5 minutes before transferring them to a wire rack to cool completely.

Nutritional Information (per serving):

Calories: 220 | **Fat:** 15g | **Carbohydrates:** 8g | **Protein:** 12g

Chapter 9: 28-Daily Nutrition Plan

Days	Breakfast	Lunch	Dinner	Desserts/Snacks
1	Protein-Rich Avocado Egg Cups	Spicy Chicken Caesar Salad	Grilled Lemon-Herb Chicken with Zucchini Noodles	Crispy Kale Chips
2	Low-Carb Berry Bliss Smoothie Bowl	Stuffed Chicken Wraps with Mushrooms and Spinach	Baked Salmon with Dill and Asparagus Spears	Spicy Avocado and Cucumber Bites
3	Spinach-Feta Omelette Roll-Ups	Creamy Broccoli Cheddar Soup	Cauliflower and Broccoli Alfredo Casserole	Spicy Roasted Almonds with Sea Salt
4	Keto-Friendly Chia Seed Pudding	Grilled Shrimp and Avocado Salad with Lime Vinaigrette	Spicy Shrimp Stir-Fry with Shirataki Noodles	Cheesy Cauliflower Bites
5	Quick and Easy Bacon Egg Muffins	Turkey and Vegetable Salad Wraps	Pesto Turkey Meatballs with Roasted Brussels Sprouts	Mediterranean Vegetable Skewers with Feta Dip
6	Greek Yogurt Parfait with Nuts and Berries	Cauliflower Bacon Chowder	Eggplant Lasagna with Ground Turkey and Spinach	Smoked Salmon Cucumber Rolls
7	Zucchini and Cheese Breakfast Casserole	Mediterranean Quinoa Salad with Feta and Olives	Lemon Garlic Butter Cod with Cauliflower Rice	Crispy Parmesan Zucchini Chips
8	Almond Flour Pancakes with Sugar-Free Syrup	Spicy Chicken and Roasted Vegetables	Stuffed Portobello Mushrooms with Spinach and Feta	Buffalo Chicken Lettuce Wraps
10	Avocado Stuffed with Smoked Salmon and Cream Cheese	Lemon Garlic Chicken Thighs with Asparagus One-Pot	Enchiladas with Ground Beef in Cabbage Wrap	Mini Caprese Salad Skewers
11	Turmeric Scrambled Eggs with Sautéed Spinach	Kale Avocado Salad with Lemon Dijon Dressing	Teriyaki Glazed Tofu Skewers with Grilled Vegetables	Sesame Ginger Sugar Snap Peas
12	Cauliflower Hash Browns with Avocado Dip	Cabbage and Sausage Skillet	Keto-Friendly Greek Salad with Grilled Chicken	Prosciutto Wrapped Asparagus Spears
13	Low-Carb Blueberry Almond Muffins	Greek Chicken Souvlaki Salad	Spaghetti Squash Carbonara with Bacon and Peas	Tomato Basil Mozzarella Tarts

Days	Breakfast	Lunch	Dinner	Desserts/Snacks
14	Coconut Chia Seed Pudding with Lime Zest	Low-Carb Egg Drop Soup with Vegetables	Lemon Butter Shrimp and Broccoli Patties	Eggplant Pizza Bites: Low-Carb and Delicious
15	Ham and Cheese Egg Muffins	Shrimp Avocado Ceviche in Lettuce Wraps	Turkey Zucchini Skillet with Creamy Tomato Sauce	Seasoned Turkey Jerky
16	Creamy Keto Coffee Smoothie	Roasted Brussels Sprouts and Bacon Salad	Grilled Swordfish Steaks with Cilantro-Lime Cauliflower Rice	Stuffed Mushrooms with Spinach and Artichokes
17	Mushroom and Swiss Cheese Frittata	Chicken and Broccoli Alfredo Zoodles	Cheesy Portobello Mushroom Caps with Ground Turkey	Goat Cheese Balls with Pistachio Crust
18	Breakfast Wrap with Avocado and Bacon	Tomato Basil Chicken from the Pot	Buffalo Chicken Salad Lettuce Wraps	Baked Parmesan Chips
19	Vanilla Almond Butter Keto Porridge	Spicy Tuna Avocado Wrap	Sesame Ginger Tofu Stir-Fry with Low-Carb Noodles	Cucumber Sushi Rolls with Smoked Salmon
21	Spicy Chicken Caesar Salad	Grilled Lemon-Herb Chicken with Zucchini Noodles	Cauliflower and Broccoli Alfredo Casserole	Peanut Butter Energy Bars with Protein Filling
22	Low-Carb Blueberry Almond Muffins	Baked Salmon with Dill and Asparagus Spears	Spicy Shrimp Stir-Fry with Shirataki Noodles	Keto-Friendly Chocolate Almond Delight Bars
23	Creamy Broccoli Cheddar Soup	Cauliflower Bacon Chowder	Pesto Turkey Meatballs with Roasted Brussels Sprouts	Low-Carb Blueberry Chia Seed Muffins
24	Grilled Shrimp and Avocado Salad	Turkey and Vegetable Salad Wraps	Eggplant Lasagna with Ground Turkey and Spinach	No-Bake Coconut Cashew Energy Bites
25	Turkey and Vegetable Salad Wraps	Mediterranean Quinoa Salad with Feta and Olives	Lemon Garlic Butter Cod with Cauliflower Rice	Banana Nut Muffins from Almond Flour
26	Cauliflower Bacon Chowder	Spicy Chicken and Roasted Vegetables	Stuffed Portobello Mushrooms with Spinach and Feta	Cinnamon Roll Protein Bars for Low-Carb Treats
27	Mediterranean Quinoa Salad with Feta and Olives	Tomato Basil Zoodle Salad	Garlic Parmesan Chicken and Vegetables from the Pan	Dark Chocolate Avocado Keto Brownies
28	Spicy Chicken and Roasted Vegetables	Lemon Garlic Chicken Thighs with Asparagus One-Pot	Enchiladas with Ground Beef in Cabbage Wrap	Lemon Poppy Seed Almond Flour Snack Bars

Chapter 10: FAQs and Additional Resources

Congratulations on reaching the final chapter of the "Low-Carb Cookbook for Beginners". By now, you've embarked on a journey to adjust your eating habits and adopt a low-carb lifestyle. As you continue your culinary adventure, it's natural to have questions and seek additional support. This chapter aims to answer some frequently asked questions and provide you with valuable resources to enhance your low-carb experience.

Frequently Asked Questions (FAQs)

Q1: Can I adapt the recipes to my dietary habits? Absolutely! The recipes in this cookbook serve as a starting point. Feel free to alter ingredients and portions according to your preferences and nutritional needs. Experimenting with flavors and textures can make your low-carb journey even more enjoyable.

Q2: Are there alternatives for certain ingredients in the recipes? Yes, of course. The cookbook introduces various low-carb substitutes for common high-carb ingredients. If you have specific dietary restrictions or allergies, you can find suitable alternatives at local health food stores or online. For personalized advice, please consult a nutritionist or dietitian.

Q3: How can I make these recipes kid-friendly? Adapting recipes for a younger audience may involve minor modifications, such as incorporating familiar flavors or creative presentations. Engage your children in the cooking process and encourage them to try new foods. Sneak vegetables into dishes or use appealing shapes to make meals more attractive.

Q4: What should I do if I'm not achieving the expected weight loss results? Each person responds differently to a change in diet. If you're not seeing the desired results, monitor your food intake, ensure you have a calorie deficit and engage in regular physical activity. Consult a healthcare professional or dietitian to address your concerns or for personalized advice.

Q5: How can I stay motivated on a low-carb diet? Staying motivated for long-term success is crucial. Set realistic goals, celebrate small victories and focus on the positive changes you're experiencing. Join a supportive community, either online or locally, to share experiences and gain inspiration from others on a similar journey.

Additional Resources

1. **Online Communities**: joining online forums and social media groups dedicated to low-carb living can provide valuable support, motivation and recipe ideas. Popular platforms include the Reddit group r/keto and various Facebook groups.

2. **Cooking Blogs and Websites**: reputable blogs and websites on low-carb cooking offer a wealth of recipes, tips and success stories. Sites like Diet Doctor, KetoConnect and All Day I Dream About Food provide a range of resources.

3. **Books and Publications**: expand your knowledge with books on low-carb living. Authors like Mark Sisson, Gary Taubes and Dr. Eric Westman offer insightful perspectives on the benefits and scientific findings of a low-carb lifestyle.

4. **Apps and Tools**: use mobile apps to track your food intake, monitor your macronutrients and discover new recipes. Apps like MyFitnessPal, Carb Manager and Cronometer can be valuable companions on your journey.

5. **Local Support Groups**: look for local support groups or meetings dedicated to the low-carb or ketogenic lifestyle. Connecting with like-minded individuals in your community can offer a sense of camaraderie and shared experiences.

Remember, every journey is unique. Experiment, stay curious and enjoy discovering what works best for you. The "Low-Carb Cookbook for Beginners" is just the beginning: a whole world of low-carb possibilities awaits to be discovered by you!

Conclusion

In summary, "The Low Carb Cookbook for Beginners" is designed to provide individuals with the tools and recipes they need to maintain a healthy, low-carb lifestyle amidst a busy schedule. We understand the challenges that busy individuals face when it comes to eating mindfully and finding time to prepare meals. This cookbook aims to simplify this process by offering a wide array of delicious, quick and easy low-carb recipes for various tastes and preferences.

Adopting a low-carb lifestyle not only supports your overall well-being but also boosts your energy levels, mental clarity and long-term health. The recipes in this cookbook are designed to be not just nutritious and satisfying, but also to integrate seamlessly into your daily work routine. We hope these recipes inspire you to prioritize your health without compromising on taste or convenience.

Remember, a low-carb lifestyle is not about deprivation but rather about making conscious and sustainable choices. Whether you're looking to manage your weight, improve your metabolic health or simply aim for a more balanced diet, "The Low Carb Cookbook for Beginners" is a valuable resource on your journey to a healthier, more vibrant life.

Thank you for choosing this cookbook as a companion on your wellness journey. May your low-carb adventure be filled with culinary delights, enhanced vitality and a renewed sense of well-being. Enjoy cooking and here's to a healthier, happier you!

Bonus

Welcome to the bonus page!

Here you can download **"The Best Guide for Dealing with Temptations"**, an unmissable management and motivational ebook that will accompany you on your low-carb diet journey.

Download it now!

SCAN THIS QR-CODE TO DOWNLOAD YOUR GREAT BONUS!

OR COPY AND PASTE THIS URL:

https://www.subscribepage.com/z7m6z2_copy9

Made in the USA
Monee, IL
25 September 2024